THE WAY OF WEALTH

To contact Frank Leyes, Author and Speaker:

Frank A. Leyes & Associates
3500 DePauw Boulevard
Pyramid II 4th Floor, Suite 2042
Indianapolis, IN 46268

Direct: 317-469-9600
Toll Free: 866-686-7589
Fax: 317-469-9601

engage@frankleyes.com

THE WAY OF WEALTH

7 STEPS TO FINANCIAL FREEDOM IN A WORLD OF ECONOMIC DEPENDENCE

FRANK LEYES

The Way Of Wealth
7 Steps To Financial Freedom In A
World of Economic Dependence

ISBN-13: 978-1492219521
ISBN-10: 1492219525

Published by Way of Wealth Enterprises,
2840 Electric Road Suite 205-A
Roanoke, VA 24018.
540-986-2686

Printed in the United States of America

This publication contains the opinions and ideas of its author and is designed to provide useful advice in regard to the subject matter covered. The author and publisher are not engaged in rendering legal, accounting, or other profes-sional services in this publication. This publication is not intended to provide a basis for action in particular circumstances without consideration by a competent professional. The author and publisher expressly disclaim any respon-sibility for any liability, loss, or risk, personal or otherwise, which is incurred as a consequence, directly or indirectly, of the use and application of any of the contents of this book.

Securities and advisory services offered through Commonwealth Financial Network®, Member FINRA/ SIPC, a Registered Investment Adviser.

*The Way of Wealth, Amazon, 8/27/13, #1 in Money Management and Retirement Planning. Amazon Best Seller rankings were calculated hourly based on number of copies sold on 8/27/13 in a chosen subcategory compared to similar books in the same subcategory. Subcategories were self-selected and some subcategories contained more books than others. Recent sales were weighted more heavily than past sales. A ranking within a subcategory is not representative of total sales or placement within Amazon's overall sales list.

*The Renegotiation of Your Retirement, Amazon, 2/28/19, #1 in Private Equity, Interest, Financial Risk Management, Health Insurance, Life Insurance, Mutual Funds, Portfolio Management, Investments, Insurance, and Real Estate. Amazon Best Seller rankings were calculated hourly based on number of copies sold on 2/28/19 in a chosen subcategory compared to similar books in the same subcategory. Subcategories were self-selected and some subcategories contained more books than others. Recent sales were weighted more heavily than past sales. A ranking within a subcategory is not representative of total sales or placement within Amazon's overall sales list.

GET YOUR

WAY OF WEALTH BONUSES

---

3 BONUSES!

- Frank's exclusive two-page Financial Roadmap
- "Parables of True Wealth" video series
- Free tele-seminar with Frank!

GET THEM HERE!

Visit www.TheWayOfWealthBook.com/Bonus

DEDICATION

This book is humbly dedicated to those individuals and institutions that have placed their trust in me over the years to help guide them through the ever-changing maze of financial complexity and along the path to financial independence. It is also dedicated to Jen, Nora, Isaiah, Daniel and Micah. My family reminds me each day that I am wealthy beyond any measure. I am eternally grateful to them, and to the One who "entrusted" them to me.

To my clients for their trust.
To my family for their love.
To my God for His redemption.

ACKNOWLEDGEMENTS

As with any substantial project, not much happens without the help of a great many people. I would like to thank the following:

My wife and family for their patience, love and support; James Gill for editing, and Jean Boles for second edit and layout; Mitch McClure and Mai Vang for video; Jeremy Ruch for research; John Riding, Ana Veljkovic and others for artwork; Mike Koenigs, Pam Hendrickson, and Chris Hendrickson for their expertise; Everett O'Keefe for project management, editing, video and artwork (not to mention the gift of friendship and encouragement throughout this process); and others for their support, kindness, feedback, and counsel.

I would also like to thank the teams at Geneos Wealth Management and Ivy Tech Community College for their ongoing support of this project and others.

CONTENTS

THE SEVEN STEPS

1. *Accept The Truth*
2. *Leverage Conviction Over Guilt*
3. *Master The Law Of Ignorance*
4. *Practice Incremental Progress*
5. *Monitor And Measure With Clarity*
6. *Maintain Perspective*
7. *Use Systems*

INTRODUCTION

"The great end of life is not knowledge, but action."
—Thomas Huxley

"Hurry up! Ring the doorbell, and get in the car before they see us."

"Oh, no! They've seen us…the front door is opening. Now, what?"

Although this exchange might appear like it came from kids trying to play a prank, this couldn't be further from the truth. These words were whispered between my wife and our children the year we were inspired to "give away Christmas." The story that follows taught me financial principles that transcend over two decades of experience as a financial advisor.

In the spirit of Christmas, my family read through a wonderful book and a Christmas classic called *Christmas Jars,* by Jason Wright. This powerful story covers one reporter's investigation of glass jars, which were packed with coins and bills and anonymously given to the needy. Sparked by this tale of kindness and generosity, we decided to "give away" Christmas that year.

Like many families, we struggle with the materialism that often takes hold of this holiday—previously known as a "Holy Day" before the word was abbreviated and lost some of its significance. As catalogs start filling the mailbox and retailers launch sales for their biggest season of the year, our children are not immune to the materialistic Christmas fever that strikes us all. However, after reading *Christmas Jars,* we elected to do Christmas much differently that year. Instead of engaging in the usual routine of buying gifts for ourselves and each other, we decided to follow the example recounted in Jason Wright's inspiring novel: we committed to find a needy family and anonymously give them gifts. This is how my family planned to "give away Christmas."

As Christmas day approached, we selected a family, purchased gifts, and devised a stealthy plan to give them away. With a van packed with my family and Christmas presents, our mission was underway. The van slowly crept along neighborhood streets to our targeted house. The kids leapt out with gifts in hand and placed them on the front porch without a sound. Then, after a brief ring of the doorbell, my children sprinted towards the vehicle for the quick getaway. Alas, before we were home free, the front door of the house flung open. Children suddenly emerged from the house, but they just didn't know what to make of the strangers who had left gifts on their porch. Looks of amazement began to surface beneath tear-filled eyes. Finally, brief dialogue led to heartfelt hugs and, of course, more tears. When Jen was asked why we would make such a gift, her reply was very humble. She said, "This gift is from a God who loves you and your family very much."

That night, my wife and children reminded me of an important lesson about wealth; there is money, and then there is "True Wealth." Money is something we all understand at some level or another. "True Wealth" is something entirely different. What I call *True Wealth* is that freedom that allows us to act out of our own financial resources to have an impact on others. It involves money only insomuch as money can be a currency of impact in this world. Money can support a charity…or a loved one. Properly managed, money allows freedom and options. True Wealth is when we can use this freedom and these options to leave a legacy and change people's lives.

Recognizing the difference between money and True Wealth is a profound lesson in life, and one that must be learned over and over again. However, it is important to understand that this life lesson in stewardship is not derived from mere information, but rather transformation. It isn't the story of *Christmas Jars* itself that brought us True Wealth, but rather taking that story to heart and acting to influence other people's lives. I assure you, my family has never been so *wealthy* as the year we "gave away Christmas."

If you are simply looking for information on wealth management, this book may not be for you. This book is designed to provide not just information but also *inspiration*. As the famous English biologist Thomas Huxley stated, *"The great end of life is not knowledge, but action."*[1] We have more information accessible to us than ever before in history. Yet, our bleak financial illiteracy is well documented, and dysfunctional money management is an out-of-control epidemic. This book will strive to deliver a recipe for change. If I cannot inspire you to *act differently*, then I have missed my mark with this work.

Great teachers throughout history have understood something very powerful about the human spirit:

- Some people learn through *principle*
- Some people learn through *parable*

In this work, I will endeavor to engage you at several levels. Parables are useful in bringing principles to life, so I have scattered several stories throughout this book. I will also instruct in plain English, as the financial world has enough complexity with its own jargon. Above all, I will make every effort to be truthful with the ultimate goal that you achieve excellence in the stewardship of your "financial wealth." Only then will you have the ultimate freedom to focus on your True Wealth.

1. Technical Education, 1877

CHAPTER ONE

The Day I Learned the True Value of Money

"Knowing what money cannot do for you will often give you the freedom to focus your attention on far more important things."

Do you remember the day you purchased your first home? What about your first car? For some, the value of money is learned by saving for their first major purchase. For others, the lesson is learned when the final credit card is paid off, which can feel as though the weight of the world has been lifted from one's shoulders. Some of us learn the true value of money by making mistakes with it.

For me, the lesson of the true value of money came when I learned what money could NOT do.

Our first pregnancy had been a joyful experience (easy for me to say!). As the third trimester proceeded, Jen was in good health and took great care of "Micah." We prayed for him, and also prayed that we would be up to the great calling and challenge of parenthood. Jen went for long morning walks, and we took parenting classes at our church and prepared a nursery to welcome him into the world. We had no way of knowing that just a few short hours after his birth, he would be welcomed to a different home.

After a completely normal pregnancy, there were complications on the day of delivery. Micah became lodged in the birth canal, and the caring hospital staff worked fervently to help deliver our little one safely into the world. A short while later, they decided we would need an emergency C-section. They took me out of the room and prepped Jen. Each second that passed seemed like hours as I waited, worried and prayed. When they finally brought me back into the room, I could feel tension and a sense of urgency in the air. During the process of repositioning Micah for the C-section, there had been more trauma. I could see concern on the doctors' faces as Micah was delivered and rushed to Neo-Natal Intensive Care (NICU). They escorted me from the delivery room and began to tend to Jen after her hours of agonizing labor and emergency surgery.

I paced, prayed, and tried to stay in touch with family members who were all concerned about the unexpected turn of events. My Pastor and dear friend stayed with me, embodying the passage that says "A friend is a friend at all times, but a brother is born for adversity." (Proverbs 17:17). From time to time, one of the staff would come in and provide an update on Micah. He had lost a great deal of blood during delivery; he was in very critical condition. They were doing everything they could to stabilize him.

Heartache, numbness, denial and hope ebbed and flowed in me with each passing moment. A short while later, a nurse approached with a sense of urgency. "Mr. Leyes," she said, "you and your wife need to come to the NICU with me *now*."

My heart sank as I realized that the nurse thought it more important and urgent for Jen to visit the NICU than to recover from her own ordeal. There are no words to describe walking into a facility like this and seeing your first child connected to a mass of tubes, IV's, respirators and other equipment in an attempt to keep him alive. The head of the NICU explained that the trauma and loss of blood had been too great for Micah.

Her last words still echo in my soul: "I don't know any other way to explain this, but some babies just have bad luck."

Sometimes words come unfiltered out of our mouths from numbness or exhaustion. Other times, it is brokenness which allows us to see clearly and to speak words beyond our own choosing.

"We don't believe in luck," I said, "God's hand has been on this child from the time he was conceived."

The next few hours gave us sacred moments to hold our newest family member. He was such a beautiful child. In spite of the trauma he had been through, he was a peaceful baby for us to cherish for this brief moment in time. Our family took turns holding him, letting him know we loved him, and ultimately, praying him into his new Heavenly home.

The name, Micah, actually means, "The prophet with beautiful feet." His precious life, only hour's long, left footprints in our hearts.

I've never seen so clearly as that day, when I looked through the tears of brokenness. That day, I understood the limits of what money can and can't do. The difference between money and "true wealth" had never been more apparent.

When you get to the place where you realize the limits of what money can do for you, there is a feeling that may surprise you: *freedom.* You see, there is often little use in anguishing about events we cannot change. Yes, you and I may experience deep, abiding sorrows in our lives. But often times, nothing can be done to change them. The limits we encounter, the things we find we cannot change, can actually bring about a freedom to focus on areas in which we have some control. The same is true in regards to money. Knowing what money *cannot* do for you will often give you the freedom to focus your attention on far more important things. Such is one of many lessons we learned from our short time with Micah.

As you take steps in the stewardship of your financial resources, be mindful of the need to also be a good steward of those things that are eternal. These things will last far longer than money.

CHAPTER TWO

We've Lost Our Way

"A democracy cannot exist as a permanent form of government. It can only exist until the voters discover that they can vote themselves money from the public treasury."

Arelia Margarita Taveras was a bright and talented TV commentator and attorney. She also liked to gamble, and tragically, developed a gambling problem. She did not know when to stop, and didn't just use her own money.

Ms. Taveras formed a habit of gambling in Atlantic City, where she would go days on end without sleeping or eating just so she could stay at the tables. Her losses amounted to over $1 million. She lost her law practice, apartment, her parents' home, and owed the IRS $58,000. She also admitted to dipping into her clients' escrow accounts.

Amazingly, Ms. Taveras later filed a $20 million racketeering lawsuit in federal court against the casinos! Read her comments, and see if you hear a problem that is plaguing our society:

"They knew I was going for days without eating or sleeping. I would pass out at the tables. **They had a duty to take care of me...**"[2]

Although it was *her* choice to gamble, and though it was *her* choice steal from her parents, and though it was *her* choice to raid her client's escrow accounts, it was somehow the *casino's* fault that she got into trouble. Unfortunately, Ms. Taveras is not the only person who thinks this way.

America and Americans (not to mention our peers around the world) are at a crossroads. We must either embrace personal responsibility with economic adulthood, or instead choose dependence. Dependence may not even be a strong enough term. I think there is a more accurate term, one rarely used these days, but perhaps more graphically descriptive: bondage. Regardless of which term we use, financial dependence or financial bondage, both terms refer to anyone or any group that is dependent upon someone else for financial viability. Whether we are discussing health care reform, social security or union retirement plans, if

---

2. Los Angeles Times. "Compulsive gambler hits casinos with suit." March 09, 2008. http://articles.latimes.com/2008/mar/09/nation/na-gamble9 (accessed July 16, 2013)

we really perceive that it is someone else's responsibility to take care of us, we are dealing with a dangerous illusion. And unfortunately, in today's society, more and more people feel that someone else is on the hook to take care of them.

Consider this: the government has no money of its own; it has only what it collects from taxpayers. The social security "trust" (a term which has about the same credibility as "Big Foot" or "The Loch Ness Monster") has no money of its own; it has only what it collects from citizens via payroll taxes, less what the government systematically borrows every day. Unions have no money of their own; their resources are limited to the funds they raise from dues or other political activities. Health insurance companies have no funds of their own; they collect premiums from the insured, plus or minus earnings on their reserves. And yet, many people seem to believe that these institutions *do* have their own money and can afford to take care of them.

The notion that "someone else" can take care of us is based on myths perpetuated over the past several decades. Because of these myths, we have lost our compass of personal responsibility and accountability.

Take a look at Paris to see a reflection of where this mistaken belief can lead us. In mid- 2010, there was a rash of strikes across France, which resulted in cancelled flights and business closures as a collective protest swept across the country. What was the focus of this protest? The French government had the gall to recommend that the retirement age be increased...**from 61 to 62!**[3] (Germany has recently increased its retirement age from 65 to 67.) The protesters in France were apparently not interested in any of the following inconvenient facts:

- Demographic trends are showing that people are living longer in retirement than previous generations, and for more years than the system was designed to support.

- Investment returns over the past decade have been woefully short of projections.

- Bailouts, which resulted from the European debt crisis, have strained the cash flow and tax structures of European governments.

Here in the United States, there have also been waves of protests in recent years. Some protests have been about collective bargaining in "right to work" states. Other protests have been about the perceived inequities in our capitalistic society. The Tea Party movement has generated protests based on fears about the amount of wealth the government has to redistribute to continue taking care of those who can't, or won't, take care of themselves.

---

3. NBC News. "France raises retirement age despite protests." November 10, 2010. http://www.nbcnews.com/id/40103988/ns/world_news-europe/t/france-raises-retirement-age-despite-protests (accessed July 16, 2013).

Analyzing these protests is beyond the scope of this book; I merely observe the emotions that seem to be brewing underneath the surface. There is fear about the implications of change and anger towards both the government and those individuals and institutions that seem compromised by special interests.

By the way, the largest special interest group may surprise you. It is the American people. Forty-seven percent (47%) of Americans pay no Federal Income Taxes.[4] Forty-eight percent (48%) of Americans receive some form of subsidy or benefit from the government.[5]

I am not judging the people on either side of the equation. Rather, I am observing that the current trends are economically unsustainable. We either change course and do everything we can to re-engage an environment of personal responsibility or head down the road of national bankruptcy, such as we see going on in Europe.

---

4. Goldstein, Jacob, and Lam Thuy Vo. "The 47 Percent, In One Graphic." *Planet Money: The Economy Explained* (blog), September 18, 2012. http://www.npr.org/blogs/money/2012/09/18/161337343/the-47-percent-in-one-graphic (accessed July 16, 2013).
5. Murray, Sara. "Nearly Half of U.S. Lives in Household Receiving Government Benefits." *Real Time Economics: Economic insight and analysis from the Wall Street Journal* (blog), January 17, 2012. http://blogs.wsj.com/economics/2012/01/17/nearly-half-of-u-s-lives-in-household-receiving-government-benefits/ (accessed July 16, 2013).

The True State of the Union

The total debt of the U.S. now exceeds $52,900 *per citizen.*[6] And you were worried that your mortgage was the only thing under water? During the time you read this page, we will add over $5 million of debt. What happens when the game of "musical debt chairs" stops? (Hint…ask Greece.)

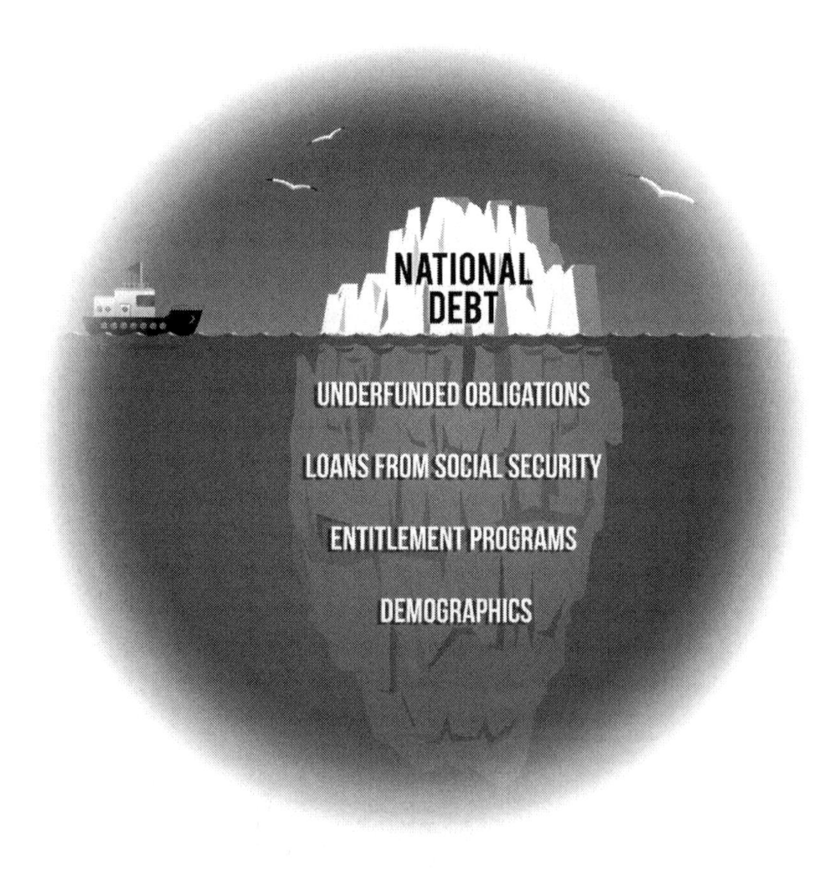

6. "U.S. National Debt Clock." Last modified July 16, 2013. Accessed July 16, 2013. http://www.brillig.com/debt_clock/.

A *Baltimore Sun* article by Eileen Ambrose quoted a statistic from the *Employee Benefits Research Institute* stating that the average 401(k) account balance for participants in their sixties is 144,000.[7] At 4% withdrawal rate this would generate only $5,760 per year in retirement, leaving a huge shortfall.

"Facts are stubborn things; and whatever may be our wishes, our inclinations, or the dictates of our passion, they cannot alter the state of facts and evidence."

John Adams,[8] 2nd American President

Social Security

But what about Social Security? In 2009, the Office of the Chief Actuary of the Social Security Administration calculated that Social Security has unfunded obligations exceeding $15 trillion (just Social Security, not the entire federal government).[9]

---

7. Ambrose, Eileen. "The 401(k) turns 30." *The Baltimore Sun*, March 06, 2011. http://articles.baltimoresun.com/2011-03-06/business/bs-bz-ambrose-401k-20110306_1_traditional-pensions-ted-benna-savings-plan (accessed July 16, 2013).

8. Adams, John. "*Argument in Defense of the Soldiers in the Boston Massacre Trials,*" *December 1770. US Diplomat & Politician* (1735 - 1826).

9. Goss, Stephen C. "The Future Financial Status of the Social Security Program." *U.S. Social Security Administration office of Retirement and Disability Policy*, August 2010. http://www.ssa.gov/policy/docs/ssb/v70n3/v70n3p111.html (accessed July 16, 2013).

Depending on which study one reads, it is estimated that Social Security will only be able to sustain 74% of current benefit levels between 2023 and 2036. To put this simply, this means that the Social Security Administration may only be able to pay you 74% of what you have been promised. Does your retirement plan allow a cushion in the event of a 26% reduction in income?

For those who espouse the notion of "Don't worry. We have plenty of time to fix the system," consider the following:

- In 2013, "Sequestration" kicked in. Sequestration was an across-the-board reduction in spending of approximately 2% (though in some cases it would be more accurate to call it a decrease in the rate of increase rather than a true "cut"). This took place as a consequence of Washington's inability to come up with a budget agreement. This miniscule reduction from our out-of-control spending was referred to as some cataclysmic event. Doom and gloom prophesies abounded. This causes me to wonder: if we are unable to come to terms with budget agreements that bring even modest restraint to government spending, why would we have confidence in the government's ability to restore solvency to something as large as Social Security?

- Each year that we delay addressing the shortfall in the Social Security system increases the severity of the measures that will need to be taken when we do get around to it. This is like the miracle of compound interest working against us.

- The government has recently begun borrowing from the government employees' pension fund in order to help meet its uncontrollable appetite for spending.[10]

You should also know that we have already squandered our greatest opportunity to repair this entitlement program. As the largest generation in history, the Baby Boomers are, progressing through their peak earning years. The contributions into the "Social Security Trust" were *supposed* to have created a surplus. This surplus was to help the program remain viable for decades to come. Instead, a government with a voracious appetite for spending systematically raided (they say "borrowed") the excess to meet its annual spending spree. As further evidence that we have "lost our way," ask yourself this question:

"If it is against the law for an employer to access the retirement funds of its employees, why is it permissible for the government to do so?"

Personal Savings

As of late 2011, the average American saved less than 4% of his or her income. By contrast, that number was 14.6% in May of 1975.

10. Alter, Diane. "U.S. Debt Ceiling: Government "Borrows" Pension Funds to Avoid Default." *Money Morning: Your Daily Map to Financial Freedom,* January 16, 2013. http://moneymorning.com/2013/01/16/u-s-debt-ceiling-government-borrows-pension-funds-to-avoid-defaul/ (accessed July 16, 2013).

If you think the current rate is bad, consider that for much of the past ten years, the national savings rate was *negative*! While the 4% number may be a recent improvement, it is woefully inadequate for anyone wanting a shred of financial independence.

Home Mortgages

In the years leading up to 2008, the United States experienced record home-ownership rates. A building frenzy ensued as demand increased, and the price of homes skyrocketed. Many people found themselves in envious equity positions in their homes. But, as of April 2013, approximately 25% of all U.S. homes had negative equity.[11] This is in spite of an extended period of historically low interest costs. Typically, with lower borrowing costs, one might anticipate greater home equity. Not in this economic environment.

11. Zillow. "The U.S. Housing Crisis: Where are home loans underwater?" Last modified May 2013. Accessed July 16, 2013. http://www.zillow.com/visuals/negative-equity/.

Student Loans

To top it off, we can see another economic "bubble" forming in the area of student loans. In 2012, the total amount of student loan debt crossed the $1 trillion mark and now exceeds the balance Americans owe on their credit cards. It is estimated that two-thirds of college seniors will graduate with debt, at an average balance of over $25,000 each. There was a time where such student loan balances were limited to budding physicians and attorneys, but now students in less high-dollar majors are incurring these substantial debts too.

What about the "return" on that investment; the investment in a college degree? For now, these graduates are coming into a stagnant economy with high unemployment. Also, older workers are remaining employed longer than in previous decades, restricting the availability of open positions. These factors don't make one's investment in a college education a bad idea. However, they give us pause to consider the continued amassing of mind-numbing levels of debt along the way.

Words of Wisdom

Consider these words, penned over 200 years ago. While there is some controversy over the source, they ring true nonetheless:

A democracy cannot exist as a permanent form of government. It can only exist until the voters discover that they can vote themselves money from the public treasury. From that moment on, the majority always votes for the candidates promising the most money from the public treasury, with the result that a democracy always collapses over loose fiscal policies, followed by a dictatorship. The average age of the world's great civilizations has been 200 years. These nations have progressed through the following sequence:

From bondage to spiritual faith;

From spiritual faith to great courage;

From courage to liberty;

From liberty to abundance;

From abundance to selfishness;

From selfishness to complacency;

From complacency to apathy;

From apathy to dependency; and,

From dependency back to bondage."

And let us not forget a compelling quote from Benjamin Franklin that echoes a parallel caution. Franklin was approached and asked about the type of government these visionaries had just formed.

"Dr. Franklin, what have you given us?" "Madam, we have given you a Republic, if you can keep it!"

—Benjamin Franklin (1787)

Consider this your personal invitation to join a quiet movement. Because of the limited resources of today, an overall decay in personal financial habits and exaggerated promises of yesterday, there is a great need to engage in your own Way of Wealth.

Engaging your Way of Wealth will require the abandonment of some long-held financial paradigms, as well as the renewed mastery of others. This quiet movement is an awakening to the reality of personal responsibility. It is, ultimately, the only path to freedom. And along the journey, you may discover or re-engage with the liberating perspective of what money can and cannot do.

CHAPTER THREE

Re-Negotiating Retirement

President Obama recently signed into law a measure that "will let companies contribute billions of dollars less to their worker's pension funds…"

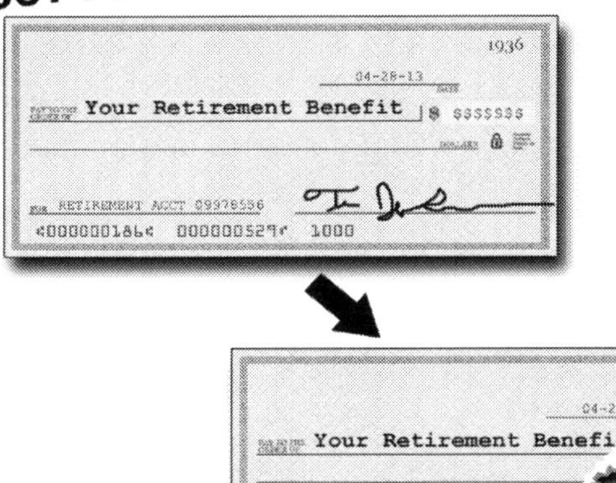

Consider this scenario. Let's imagine first that your mortgage payment has come down 20% over the last 10 years. This is the result of re-financing (perhaps multiple times) during this extended period of historically low interest rates. Congratulations! That's the good news.

But then you receive a letter from your pension plan (or Social Security), which states that your monthly pension benefit is also being reduced by 20%, effective next month. The letter offers a few explanations for the reduction in promised benefits:

"A significant portion of our pension assets have been invested in mortgage-backed and fixed-income securities. These investments have underperformed their assumptions and historic earnings averages. In addition, a portion of our pension fund has been invested in the stock market. Over the past decade, the equities markets have also underperformed the assumed rates of return and historical averages. The combination of these two factors leaves us with no alternative but to reduce your benefits."

In other words, while you are fortunate to save 20% on your mortgage payments each month, the provider of your retirement income has experienced a similar-sized reduction in revenue. This has occurred because the same forces that have pushed down your interest rates have also forced down the amount of money that your pension plan earns on investments.

Situations like this one are becoming common now that the Great Recession has shaken the foundations of our financial system. Many retirement plans that were tied to equities are now underfunded; consequently, these plans are forced to reduce benefits. People facing these cuts often wonder if there are immediate solutions to this problem. Here are a few they suggest...and the sad truths that are exposed.

1. Solution #1: Maintain benefit levels by increasing taxes or union dues.

This solution is not feasible for demographic reasons. The sheer concentration of retirees (the many), as compared with the substantially smaller number of those still working (the few), makes this approach unworkable.

2. Solution #2: Maintain current benefit levels by reducing benefits payable to future retirees?

This would also not solve the problem because the number of current retirees receiving pension benefits is twice the number of those still working and progressing toward retirement. In addition, the gap between current assets and benefits compared with the previous assumptions is simply too great. Postponing these adjustments could potentially bankrupt the pension fund.

Welcome to your future. The same economics that saved you money on your mortgage are also responsible for your decreased pension. Condolences, this is the bad news, and it gets worse from here.

- In 2012, approximately 4 out of 5 pension plans were underfunded.[12]

- The average pension plan carries just 76.9% of the assets needed to meet its obligations.[13]

- In 2009, it was estimated that the Illinois Pension Fund only had assets covering 50.6% of promised benefits.[14]

- The Pension Benefit Guarantee Corp (which "insures" pension plans at taxpayer expense) now has control of over 4,300 plans covering 1.5 million individuals. By its own estimates, it has a 91% chance of becoming insolvent by 2032.[15] Place this projection alongside the context of Social Security only being in a position to pay 74% of its benefits by 2036 and we have a retirement crisis of epic proportion.

---

12. Fram, Alan. "New law gives employers break on pension payments." *The Roanoke Times,* sec. Business, July 10, 2012.
13. Zeiler, David. "Retirement Nightmare: Underfunded Pensions Want to Chop Your Benefits by 60%." *Money Morning: Your Daily Map to Financial Freedom,* April 17, 2013. http://moneymorning.com/2013/04/17/retirement-nightmare-underfunded-pensions-want-to-chop-your-benefits-by-60/ (accessed July 16, 2013).
14. Skarbeck, Ken. "SKARBECK: Expect more battles over public pensions." *IBJ.com.* http://www.ibj.com/skarbeck-expect-more-battles-over-public-pensions/PARAMS/article/22327 (accessed July 16, 2013).
15. Boak, Josh. "How Congress Is Putting Pension Plans At Serious Risk." *Business Insider,* April 15, 2013. http://www.businessinsider.com/congress-putting-your-pension-at-risk-2013-4 (accessed July 16, 2013).

Consider the plight of the U.S. Postal Service. Among its many challenges, it, too, has a retirement system that is woefully underfunded. A recent *Wall Street Journal* article on these financial challenges stated that "Without Congressional action, [the U.S.P.S.] will be unable to make a $5.5 billion payment into the health benefits fund for retirees."[16] The irony in this statement is the reflection that we believe Washington has the solution to all of our economic problems. Nonetheless, Congress cannot change the laws of economics.

If one needs an example of how politics and economics are related to one another, consider the following case in point. In his October 2009 article, "Steep Losses Pose Crisis for Pensions," *Washington Post* Reporter David Cho explains how the city of Philadelphia issued a dire warning to state legislators. When faced with the necessity of adding to their public pension fund, Philadelphia actually issued an ultimatum: "Allow the city to take a two-year break from contributing to its pension system, or Philadelphia will lay off 3,000 workers and cut sanitation and public safety services."[17]

Cho delivered further perspective on the problem:

---

16. Levitz, Jennifer. "Post Office Might Miss Retirees' Payment." *The Wall Street Journal.* http://online.wsj.com/article/SB10000872396390444097904577535322022316422.html (accessed July 16, 2013).
17. Cho, David. "Steep Losses Pose Crisis for Pensions." *The Washington Post,* sec. Business, October 11, 2009. http://articles.washingtonpost.com/2009-10-11/business/36837729_1_pension-funds-public-pension-pension-managers (accessed July 16, 2013).

> After losing about $1 Trillion in the markets, state and local governments are facing the devil's choice: Either slash retirement benefits or pursue high return investments that come with high risk.
>
> The problem isn't limited to public pension funds; many corporate pension funds have lost so much ground that they are also pursuing riskier investments. **And they too, could become a taxpayer burden if they cannot meet their obligations and are taken over by the federal Pension Benefit Guarantee Corp.[18] (emphasis added)**

On the date of Cho's article, the stock market was wrapping up one of its worst decades in history. While most pension funds assume investments will earn between 7.5 and 8%, the S&P 500 Index had just finished a 10-year period where it had declined 32%.

The gap between the promised benefits of yesterday and the resources of today is accelerating toward a point of no return. The question may not be "*Do* we raise taxes or lower benefits." Rather, it very well may be, "*how much* do we raise taxes and lower benefits."

With the stock market and fixed income earnings well below assumptions, retiree longevity well beyond expectations and pension funds underfunded by trillions of dollars, one may

18. *ibid.*

ask, "What are we doing to fix the situation?" President Obama recently signed into law a measure that "will let companies contribute billions of dollars *less* to their worker's pension funds…"[19] The motivation for the ludicrous bill seems to be to reduce the financial pressure for companies who are behind on funding their pensions. The thinking is if we don't lighten up the pressure, these companies might freeze or terminate their pension plans. This is a step backwards on "The Way of Wealth."

Consider yourself warned. While no one has sent you a letter telling you your benefits have been cut by 20%, this situation may very well be an impending reality. If you want further verification, take a look at the disclosure on your Social Security statement of benefits (now available online at www.ssa.gov). The disclaimer states that the "trust fund" will only be able to pay 76% of current benefits. This is just the first warning. Who will heed that warning? And how? In the chapters ahead, you will see that personal responsibility is the only path to freedom.

---

19. Fram, Alan. "New law gives employers break on pension payments." *The Roanoke Times*, sec. Business, July 10, 2012.

CHAPTER FOUR

Watch Out For The Experts!

"A politician needs the ability to foretell what is going to happen tomorrow, next week, next month, and next year. And to have the ability afterwards to explain why it didn't happen."
—Winston Churchill

April 25, 2011 (Fox News interview)[20]
Peter Barnes (reporter): "Is there a risk that the United States could lose its AAA credit rating? Yes or no?"
Timothy Geithner (Treasury Secretary): "No risk of that."
Peter Barnes: "No risk?"
Timothy Geithner: "No risk."

August 6, 2011 (Reuters headline)[21]
"United States loses prized AAA credit rating from S&P"

---

20. Weil, Jonathan. Bloomberg, "Geithner Downgrades His Own Credibility to Junk: Jonathan Weil." Last modified April 20, 2011. Accessed July 16, 2013. http://www.bloomberg.com/news/2011-04-20/geithner-downgrades-his-own-credibility-to-junk-jonathan-weil.html.
21. Brandimarte, Walter, and Daniel Bases. Reuters, "United States loses prized AAA credit rating from S&P." Last modified August 06, 2011. Accessed July 16, 2013. http://www.reuters.com/article/2011/08/06/us-usa-debt-downgrade-idUSTRE7746VF20110806.

Let me get right to the main point of this chapter:

Everyone giving you financial advice has an angle, a motivation, something that is in it for them.

Obviously, since I am writing this book, I do not inherently think everyone who writes financial literature has a conflict of interest with your financial future. Just because someone is on television or the radio doesn't mean that they are out to undermine your path to financial security. Nonetheless, it is vitally important that you develop a growing level of discernment, and this can come from understanding the interests and motives behind financial publications and media.

For example:

- The primary motivation of an author or financial publication is to get you to buy a book or subscribe to the publication.

- The driving force behind financial television and radio is *ratings*. While the radio or TV station might claim it only wants you to "tune in" because you won't get such insightful information and perspective anywhere else, the *real* reason is ratings, which directly affect the station's advertising revenue.

- There is no such thing as an impartial economic or government source for financial information. Instead, there is a general bias that needs to be considered.

- Even a financial professional who offers a "Free Review" has a motivation for compensation. These professionals know that for every so many free consultations, a certain percentage of individuals may become clients. And there is nothing inherently wrong with this approach as long as everyone is aware of the process and motivation.

Since every source of information has some kind of agenda or self-interest, your goal is not to try to find sources that are completely unbiased. Such sources don't exist. Instead, you need to find sources whose self-interests are consistent with your own. And you shouldn't be trying to find someone who is not out for their own best interest. Your job is to find reliable sources of sound financial information and then develop *wisdom* for your unique circumstances. To put it plainly:

- Find someone who is willing to *admit* his or her self-interest

- Confirm that it lines up with *your* self-interest.

Regardless of your sources of financial advice, remain mindful of the motivation and beware of the accompanying potential blind spots. We find classic examples of this in statements made by government officials. When representatives of the Federal Reserve speak, there is a motivation toward wanting to keep the economy moving along and consumers propped up with a sense of confidence. Here are just a few examples:

"I don't see any significant recession or depression in the offing."
-George Humphrey,
U.S. Secretary of Treasury; July 1957

(The recession of 1957 began the next month)

"This promises to be the most prosperous year in our history."
-Robert Anderson,
U.S. Secretary of Treasury; April 1960

(The recession of 1960 began THAT MONTH!)

"We do not expect significant spillovers from the subprime market to the rest of the economy or the financial system."
-Ben Bernanke, Chairman of the Federal Reserve; May 2007

(You don't own a calculator with enough digits on it to calculate how wrong this comment was!)

"The only function of economic forecasting is to make astrology look respectable."

—John Kenneth Galbraith

With the level of media overload that we receive on a daily basis, we understand the Federal Reserve's desire to focus on the positive. Just be careful about making a decision to expand your business, buy a new car or upgrade to that new house based on false confidence coming from the Federal Reserve. If you rely upon the "The Fed," you may have a rude surprise.

Financial publications are also not immune to their own interests either. Their main goal is to keep us reading and subscribing, and they will often go to absurd lengths to get people to read. Case in point: the February 2007 issue of *Money Magazine* contained an editor's note entitled "You CAN Pick the Best Funds." In that article, however, was the contradictory nugget: "Savvy investors and honest advisors know that it's impossible to identify top performing funds in advance."

Clearly, this is an example of using a headline or cover story to entice people to purchase the magazine. However, *Money* admits that no one has the ability to identify top-performing funds in advance. Research and marketing firms invest millions of dollars each year in analytical software solutions designed to help advisors and the public find top-performing investments just before they take flight.

Yet, even with such amazing tools these firms can give dangerous advice. In an article posted by the *Wall Street Journal*, Jennifer

Levitz points out that, "John Coumarianos, an analyst for Chicago-based mutual-fund researcher Morningstar Inc., suggests that a retiree have no more than 20% in stock exposure."[22]

This dysfunctional advice from an "expert" was published in *The Wall Street Journal* on December 1, 2008. The market was in free fall that day and actually lost over 679 points to close at 8,149. The media subsequently pronounced that the U.S. economy was officially in a recession. Generally speaking, Morningstar is a trusted name among those who provide research of the investment industry. However, this piece of expert advice, and the timing with which it was delivered, could not have been worse.

Follow me for a minute. Imagine being a typical retiree with an investment portfolio of 60% stocks and 40% bonds, which is not uncommon. It's December 1, 2008, and you are terribly stressed because of the financial meltdown going on around you. You read this piece of advice at the end of the day and decide you can't take it anymore. Based on the advice you read from Mr. Coumarianos, you reallocate your portfolio and reduce your stock holdings from 60% to 20%. You go to bed that night feeling somewhat comforted that you have minimized future losses and followed an expert's advice.

---

22. Levitz, Jennifer. "What Do You Do Now? Rethinking risk and 'tax-loss selling' are smart moves for battered fund investors." *The Wall Street Journal.* http://online.wsj.com/article/SB122722136606545749.html (accessed July 16, 2013).

Now, fast forward in time to May 2013 with the market at all-time highs above 15,000. If you followed the advice of this Morningstar analyst, you missed out on the subsequent recovery on the stocks you sold!

"Nobody can predict interest rates, the future of the economy or the stock market. Dismiss all such forecasts..."

—Peter Lynch

My point is this: you alone can determine the amount of risk that is appropriate for your portfolio. Better yet, you in concert with a financial professional can make an even better determination. The "experts" who irresponsibly recommend less risk ignore certain realities which influence how much risk is actually appropriate. For those of you in a position to retire, today's reality is quite different than that of previous generations. For instance, you may need a retirement plan measured in decades rather than years. In this case, consider invest-ments that have historically demonstrated an ability to outpace inflation and taxes, and then determine what your balance of risk should be.

INFLATION?

If you are a "Buy and Hold" investor, stick with your model and keep in mind the words attributed to Warren Buffett: "The secret to making money in stocks is in not getting scared out of them." If you are an investor who uses a more active approach to asset allocation, then follow the discipline of your system and ignore alarmist experts. Remain more focused on and committed to your goals than you are distracted by the crisis of the day.

How to Evaluate an Investment:

- **Past performance**
- **Expenses**
- **How it fits in your Investment Strategy**
- **Continuity of management**
- **Risk**

Watch Out For Sales Pitches

We live in the information age. For the first time in history, we have more information at our fingertips about any subject, including investments, than we could process in a lifetime. While the value of all of this information remains in question, the abundance, even excess of it, is obvious. However, much of the information we have available comes attached to advertisements. Billions of dollars are spent each year on financial advertising, both directly to the public, to financial advisors and *through experts.* The over-abundance of advertising in the financial sector generates a great amount of false hype for investors, as the following example illustrates.

Assume you are watching TV and you get this pitch from a commercial:

"You should place your money with my firm because we know something about Microsoft stock (or fill in the stock of your choice) that no one else does. We know when it is mispriced, when to buy it and when to sell it."

15 seconds later, you see another commercial from another company:

"You should invest your money with my firm because we have the inside scoop on Microsoft! We really know when it is mispriced, when to buy it and when to sell it."

Now, here are a couple things to consider: First, if one of these firms really did know something about a stock that no one else did, this would be called *insider information*. Acting upon this "secret information" would be *insider trading*, which happens to be illegal. Second, if this information were truly so valuable, wouldn't they use it for themselves instead of you?

Sales pitches like these come from a variety of entities:

- Mutual Fund Companies
- Separate Account Managers
- Hedge Fund Managers
- Financial Advisors
- Financial Experts

Does all of this advertising work? It depends on how you interpret the question. Historical studies of investors chasing hot funds (those with superior recent performance records) would seem to validate that advertising does ultimately convince people to invest.

We can also see from the empirical data that money tends to flow into a fund following periods of *over-performance*. This is a period when the fund performs better than equivalent funds. Once this period of over-performance ends, money tends to come pouring out of the fund, which causes a period of *under-performance*. The sad truth is that most people tend to invest in a fund too late, after its period of great growth, and also exit too late, after the fund has given up much of its value. You may have experienced this phenomenon yourself and simply wondered if you had the "investment curse." It is almost like the investment *knows* you have put money in it, at which point it promptly retreats. Rather than focusing strictly on the PERFORMANCE of investments, let's be mindful of the BEHAVIOR of the investor. It may not be that you "have" the investment curse. Rather, you may "be' the investment curse.

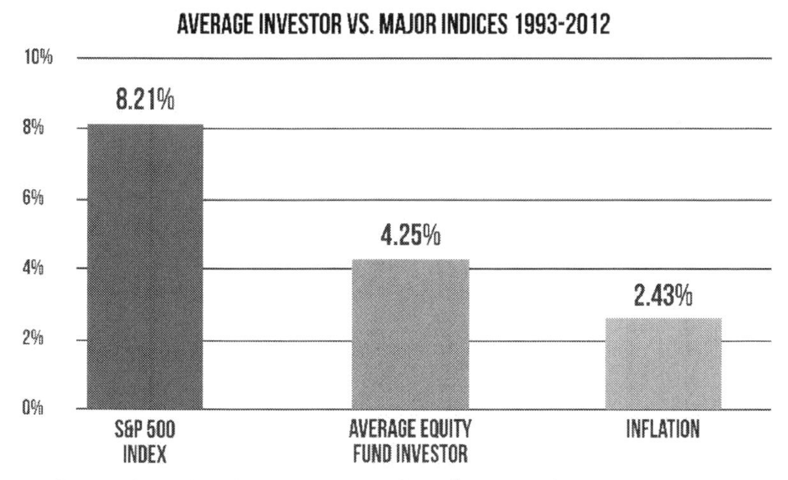

Source: *DALBAR study, Quantitative Analysis of Investor Behavior (QAIB), 03/2013*

There are many reasons maintaining a superior-performing fund is hard. It can be difficult to manage funds with massive amounts of new investments coming in. There is also a challenge of being nimble when dealing with larger bases of assets and the simple nature of cycles in investment performance. Any position, strategy or philosophy that takes a stance capable of out-performing during one period is also, by definition, equally capable of under-performing during the next cycle.

This may beg the question, "Do we ignore the performance of investments?" Of course not. However, be aware that performance is merely one criteria of a sound investment.

Other criteria include:

- Expenses (not merely the expenses to manage the fund, but also additional fees.)
- How the investment fits into the overall strategy or plan.
- Continuity of the advisor or firm delivering the plan.

More than anything, do *not* naively follow the often self-serving advice of so-called experts, whether they show up on CNBC, PBS, infomercials or special newsletter services. One of the greatest skills we can develop in this age of 'information obesity' is to choose to selectively IGNORE vast amounts of entertainment and information that would distract us from our goals.

Never take financial or investment advice from someone who is not accountable to you for how it performs in the context of helping you reach your financial and life goals.

Before we leave this chapter, I would like to share with you a powerfully effective application of this concept.

How To Make a Prospective Financial Advisor Sink or Swim

If you are interviewing a prospective financial advisor or wealth manager, ask these questions to cut through self-interest and determine if you can really trust your advisor:

QUESTION 1: May I see a copy of your own personal investment strategy to see if you believe in these investments enough to own them yourself?

This is truly one of those "moment of truth" questions. You should be on the lookout for changes in body language, defensiveness, eye contact and the willingness of the advisor to prove his or her convictions. However, be aware that the advisor may have legitimate reasons for not owning the exact same investments they recommend to you. Lots of factors can and should affect the advisor's own investment strategies. These include:

- The advisor's age
- The advisor's goals
- The advisor's life circumstances
- The advisor's ability to tolerate risk

All of these should be taken into account when considering the advisor's own investment portfolio. A 35-year-old advisor would be expected to have a portfolio that has a greater growth emphasis than a prospective 65-year-old client who is looking to retire. Generally, you want to be on the lookout for a blatant conflict that is not attributable to age, goals and life circumstances. For example:

- The advisor has all of his or her money in individual stocks while recommending mutual funds for you.

- The advisor is heavily invested in cash, bonds and conservative investments while telling you to ride out a downturn.

- The advisor has a personal portfolio that is void of the money managers, strategies or philosophies being recommended to you.

It is perfectly appropriate for the advisor to omit the dollar amounts in his or her portfolio. You aren't asking the question to see how much money the advisor has accumulated. Rather, you are gauging the advisor's convictions to see if he or she feels so strongly about the advice given to you that he or she will follow it personally.

QUESTION 2: Do the managers of these recommended investments place their own funds into the portfolio they are managing?

This is important. Consider this from *Morningstar Advisor Magazine*:[23]

- 47% of U.S. stock funds report no manager ownership.

- 61% of foreign stock funds report no manager ownership.

---

23. "Manager's Investment Secrets Revealed." *Morningstar Advisor Magazine*, Fall 2008.

- 66% of taxable bond funds report no manager ownership.
- 71% of balanced funds report no manager ownership.
- 80% of municipal bond funds report no manager ownership.

-*Morningstar Advisor Magazine*, Fall 2008, "Manager's Investment Secrets Revealed."

Notably, there are occasions where it may not be appropriate for a manager to own his or her fund, such as one managing a municipal bond for a municipality where they do not reside. But for the most part, these statistics reveal a staggering lack of vested interest in the funds being managed. If you ever find an advisor or fund manager unwilling to invest in his or her own strategies or fund, *STAY AWAY!*

Remember that expertise about a given subject is only part of the puzzle. What good does it do to work with the world's greatest expert if he or she does not have your best interest, or your mutual interests, at heart? You wouldn't want to take your car to a dishonest mechanic. Similarly, don't take your investments to experts who don't pass this integrity test.

Keep in mind that you are looking for advice that is accurate and trustworthy, from a source that *shares* your interests. Make this your goal, ask tough questions, and you won't go wrong. And, do not expect every recommendation of the advisor to be a resounding success. There are times, such as those in our current markets, when certain fundamentals don't seem to apply. If a strategy is implemented with sound conviction in its ability to help you along your Way of Wealth and it does not work out, move on. Having many eggs in many baskets can serve you well…and so can having realistic expectations.

Now that we've taken a look at how self-interest impacts the usefulness of financial information, resources and advice, you may be wondering about my own interests.

I do not write for a living, and thankfully so. With each page I write, my respect for those who do this for a living increases. The primary purpose of the book is to help people I cannot reach in person or accept as individual clients. This book is also designed to be a helpful resource for those who hear me speak and need to dig further into the philosophies and concepts I share. It can also serve as a reference point for those who engage the services of another advisor, or even choose to navigate their Way of Wealth on their own. While I am obviously not giving the book away, most books are far from money makers (as any honest author or publisher will disclose!). Ultimately, this book is about planting seeds that go beyond the individuals I may work with on a personal basis. There is an avalanche of garbage that will compete for your financial attention. A great deal of it is promoted by sources with little or no real-world experience or credentials in helping people implement and apply sound financial principles. Ironically, because of my licenses and professional credentials, virtually every word of this book will be scrutinized before it is authorized to be published. Those individuals without such credentials have the liberty to say or print almost anything.

But I do have a self-interest here: should you find the information in this book helpful, you may wish to learn more from me through my exclusive membership site, www.mywayofwealth.com. This is a membership community where you can receive ongoing financial wisdom, distilled from the white noise of financial "experts." In addition to the frequently updated content, you will find useful financial calculators, book reviews, cutting-edge research on wealth management, overviews of potential age-specific strategies, and a community forum where you can interact with others in our membership group. We also post the specific investment models we use in the management of our individual client accounts on the site so you can have a point of reference for the management of your own investments.

My mission remains to help you with the excellent stewardship of your financial resources so you are free to focus on your True Wealth.

"So if you have not been trustworthy in handling worldly wealth, who will entrust you with true riches?"

Luke 16:11

CHAPTER FIVE

Two Kinds of People

Cycle of dependence:
Those who choose to spend first and save what's left are dependent upon those who are disciplined enough to save first and then spend.

Since I became a financial advisor in 1985, every client and prospective client that I've come into contact with fits into one of two categories. Ironically, it is not unusual for a husband and wife to be in different categories. While this can be a source of tension, it can also be an important element of balance in a marriage. This idea was first introduced to me by John Savage, one of the most successful life insurance agents in the history of the insurance industry. I met John in Toledo, Ohio during the waning years of his career and, sadly, his life. In his final years battling cancer, John had opened up his office for others to see the practices and values that led to his success.

During a presentation, John drew two circles on the board and proceeded to tell the audience, "There are only two kinds of people:"

1. There are those who SPEND FIRST, then save what's left.
2. There are those who SAVE FIRST, then spend what's left.

John's next sentence echoes as one of the most profound and succinct pieces of wisdom I have ever encountered:

> ***"The people in the first group will spend their entire lives working for the people in the second group."***

TWO KINDS OF PEOPLE

If you remember nothing else from this chapter, please remember this important concept. If someone takes the philosophy of spending what money they have earned and then saving only if some money is left over, do you believe that, at the end of the day, that person will actually save any money? And where do those people go when an opportunity, or an emergency, presents itself? They have to go to where the money is. Whether they go to a bank or credit card company, the money comes from people who have saved first and invested. If I go to the bank for a loan, utilize a credit card or take out a mortgage, the money I borrow has been made available (at a premium) by people who save. Banks, credit card companies and mortgage companies all amass capital to lend through the savings and investments of those who have the discipline and foresight to save.

What you see going on here is a cycle of dependence. Those who choose to spend first and save what's left are dependent upon those who are disciplined enough to save first and then spend. In every financial decision that we make, we should be mindful of our constant objective to move from circle #1 to circle #2.

Businesses also fall into one of the two groups listed above, and, consequently, many of them also lose touch with the importance of establishing a reserve. There is a paradox that can trap the thinking of a business owner. When times are good, they may not perceive the need for a cash reserve. However, when times are difficult, they don't have a reserve to use, *and* the ability to borrow can be restricted. We have seen the tightening of lending standards as a result of the Great Recession. This makes borrowing even more difficult during tough economic times, when businesses most need to borrow. With little or no reserves to fall back on, a business can be taken under by a seemingly small decrease in sales during a time of economic downturn.

Yes, I am aware of the excuses of why businesses don't save:

- "I can't earn any interest on short-term savings."
- "The IRS actually penalizes me if I leave too much cash in my business."
- "My shareholders and business partners are always pressuring me to utilize any available funds to grow the business rather than keep cash on the sidelines."

In response, I'll quote a piece of timeless wisdom shared from a dear friend and mentor:

"Some people make excuses...others make progress. You get to choose."

To move toward financial independence, we must accept an elevated level of personal responsibility. We must be willing to give up our excuses and become more aware of our own beliefs and daily decisions. We have a choice to make: we can make excuses… or we can make progress.

As you evaluate your own journey on your "Way of Wealth," first determine which circle describes you best. Do you spend the money you earn and only save if some is left over at the end of the month? Or do you put some money aside for savings the moment you receive it, and then learn to live on what remains afterward?

While I was profoundly affected when John told me that the people who spend first will be dependent upon the people who save first, this wasn't a new idea. In fact, these two groups of people have been recognized for thousands of years:

"…the borrower is slave to the lender." Proverbs 22:7

Don't be a slave to the lender.

It's never too late to switch circles.

CHAPTER SIX

Seven Circles and One Heart to Financial Freedom

Consider these Seven Circles and One Heart to Financial Freedom and recognize the importance of the interplay between them.

I want to introduce to you Seven Circles and One Heart to Financial Freedom. This will be a helpful framework to take the complexities of the financial world and make them simple to understand.

We've already gone over two of the Seven Circles earlier in this book. The first two circles are the two types of people that are in the world:

1. There are those who SPEND FIRST, then save what's left.

2. There are those who SAVE FIRST, then spend what's left.

With this backdrop in mind, let's explore more closely the other circles and the Heart to Financial Freedom.

The Savings Account Circle

The single most important facet of a financial plan—and this shocks most people when I say it—is the bank account. Yes, I have looked at statements lately, and I know what bank accounts are paying in the way of interest. As a matter of fact, the interest that a bank account pays is not important. The interest rate that it *keeps* us from paying *is* important. Let me explain.

A bank account is for liquid, easily accessible cash that you can use for unexpected circumstances. People who fail to save are only one major expense from debt. A person without savings who has a car breakdown, or an appliance failure, or a medical emergency will often have to resort to credit cards or other loans to pay these expenses. And these loans come at a premium cost. A few unexpected expenses and a person can himself buried in high-interest debt.

On the other hand, the person with a savings account (and money in it!) can handle unexpected expenses. This person doesn't have to incur high-cost debt at all. So you see, the value of a savings account (even one that earns little to no interest) is to keep you from having to take out loans or use credit cards, and incur the high interest rates associated with these sources.

7 CIRCLES & 1 HEART

TWO KINDS OF PEOPLE

THREE WAYS TO INVEST

SAVINGS ACCT VS TIN CAN

2%
interest

0%
interest

My clients like to remind me of the '70s when their money market accounts were paying double-digit rates of interest. What they often forget to mention is that the inflation rate was even higher. When I pull out a chart of historical inflation rates, we find that, though their bank account balance was increasing, their purchasing power was not.

The primary purpose of the savings account is to develop the discipline of setting money aside, which is critical in establishing the foundation of your financial strategy. This is the first discipline and one that cascades over into the other disciplines of investing in a well-diversified manner over time. In fact, when a client applies for a more advanced investment, I make sure that he or she has a sufficient reserve in his or her bank account to give their investment the best opportunity to earn market/optimum rates of return. It doesn't help the client if we place money into a great investment if the client has to pull some or all of that money out of the investment three months later because of a car breakdown or family emergency. Investments often have associated expenses which may be negligible if factored over time but seem more significant if money has to be unexpectedly removed from the investment just a few months later.

In the past, you may have heard people say that three to six months' income or expenses is a reasonable benchmark for a savings account. I believe that, in today's world, this number needs to reflect one year's worth of expenses. Want some explanation for this shift? Take a look at the following graph:

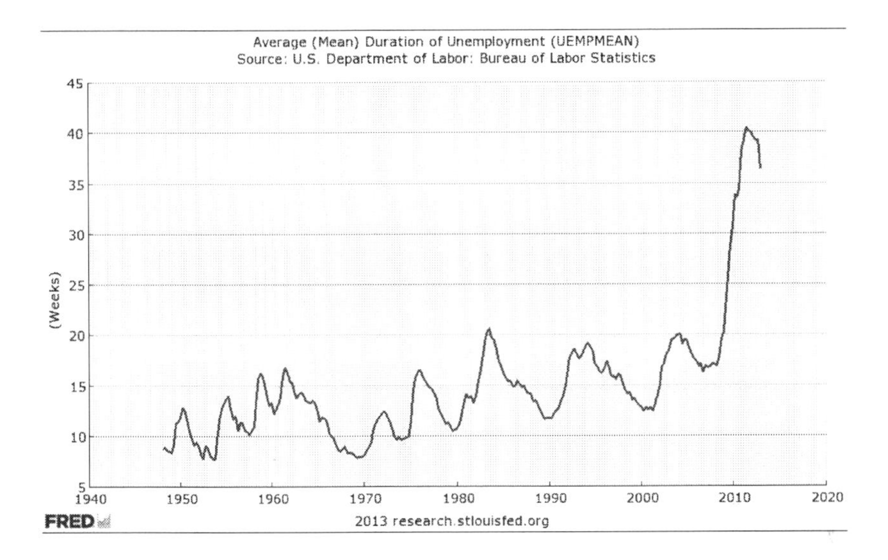

In 1948, the average person receiving unemployment was unemployed for about nine weeks. As of the writing of this book, the average person on unemployment uses that benefit for 37 weeks, a period *four times* longer than 1948. And recognize that this number reflects the *average* person on unemployment. This means that a large percentage of recipients are on unemployment for longer than 37 weeks, some much longer. And what this chart cannot show is the number of people who are unemployed but no longer receiving benefits, or are so discouraged that they are no longer looking for work. Given these numbers, you can see why I now recommend that people set aside a year of living expenses.

We're finding that economic cycles and recessions are lasting longer, and for many, the period in between jobs is growing longer as well. Therefore, it is even more important that the reserve we use in the event of emergencies can give us freedom during transition periods without unnecessary debt.

To review, you want to be certain that you utilize a bank account for the *interest it will prevent you from paying*, not for the interest it will earn you. Of course, we know that those earnings may not keep ahead of inflation consistently over time. That's where the investment circle comes in. But you can never effectively invest if you don't have savings to support you in unexpected circumstances.

The Investment Circle

The investment circle is ultimately where we want the majority of our wealth to accumulate. This may contain stocks, bonds, mutual funds, annuities, retirement accounts, commodities, precious metals, etc. These can all be parts of a diversified financial plan. The purpose of a diversified financial plan is to give your wealth the best opportunity to stay ahead of inflation as you attempt to bring a point of financial freedom to fruition.

While the first circle qualifies you for the second circle, we know that, over time, the majority of your net worth needs to be in a diversified investment portfolio. By doing this, you can combat inflation and create the future that you deserve. Ironically, many people focus almost exclusively on this circle, focusing energy on investments without properly taking care of savings, or the next circle, that of Insurance. Before we move on, consider the following chart from the highly respected firm, T. Rowe Price. It provides some general investment category guidelines for various investment purposes and time frames.

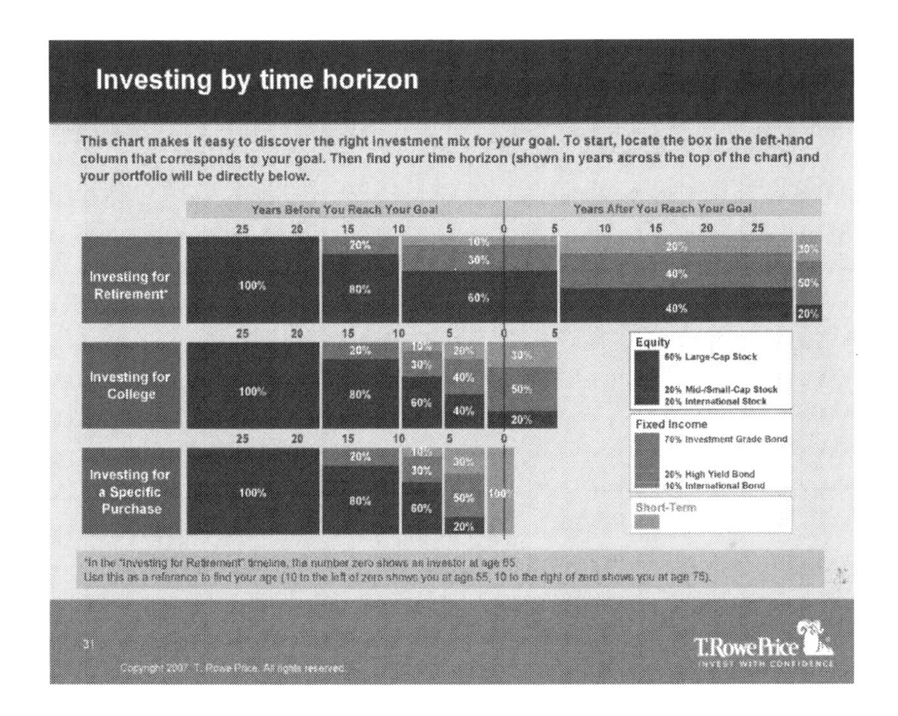

The Insurance Circle

Due to its complexity, there's much confusion about what goes on in the insurance circle. To put it simply, all insurance is designed to fulfill two primary objectives:

- Buy time
- Share risk

Disability insurance buys time for those who can't work and replaces their earnings until they can get back to work. Life insurance buys time for someone's family or dependents in the event he or she dies prematurely and leaves a financial burden on the family. Long-term care insurance buys time for someone to be able to cover the costs of long-term care without having to be deprived of one's own assets. Thus, the primary roles of the insurance circle are to share risk and buy time until a harmonized financial strategy comes to fruition.

The Bank Account and The Tin Can

Let's move our focus to the final two circles. Assume that you decide to set aside $200 a month as an investment strategy, and you're going to do this every month for five years. There are two options for where that $200 a month will go. The first option is the bank, which will pay you 2% interest on your savings (I know, the 2% is purely hypothetical, but you'll get my point in a moment). The second option is a tin can, which will pay you 0% interest. For a five-year period, you're going to save $200 a month in either the bank account or the tin can. At the end of the five-year period, where do you believe most people will have the most money?

BANK VS. TIN CAN

2%
interest

0%
interest

Before you answer, there's a catch.

The bank account has easy access. You can stop by your branch, use your ATM card, bank by phone, or even transfer funds online. The tin can, however, operates a little differently. The tin can only opens up for the $200 contribution once month. You cannot get your hands on anything that's inside the tin can because it will only open for the next $200 contribution to go in. This happens every month over a five-year period.

The question is, at the end of the five-year period, in which account—the bank or tin can—would you retain the most money? Keep in mind that when money goes into the tin can, a vise clamps shut. The tin can only opens once each month in order to receive the next contribution.

I've been asking this question to clients for over 25 years, and the answer is always the same: people realize they will have more money in the tin can. When asked for an explanation, they'll say it's because they can't access the money in the tin can. Money we can access tends to be money we spend.

Looking at it more closely, tin cans have been successful tools for wealth accumulation over the decades. For years and years, home equity was a form of tin can. We paid our mortgage like a bill, and our home equity accumulated accordingly. In fact, when we made that tin can too easy to access (through easily acquired home equity loans), there was a significant decline in the real estate market. For many people, their retirement plan is another tin can. They can make contributions, but they can't access them prior to retirement (without taxes or penalties unless a loan provision exists). Some people use insurance vehicles as a tin can as well. The slow and steady tax deferred features of certain forms of permanent insurance can also serve as a tin can.

The common characteristic is that the success of a financial strategy is determined by systematic and disciplined contributions and restraining ourselves from accessing it. The rate of return is considerably less important. There is so much attention in the financial world on achieving the ideal rate of return on investments. But not enough attention is focused on the rate of savings. If we are unwilling to set aside an appropriate measure of our income, no magic formula for investing is likely to overcome this deficiency.

The Heart

Now, let's get to the heart of the matter. There is one more element to discuss, which might be the most important: the "One Heart" to Financial Freedom. Having worked with individuals and institutions since 1985, I have observed a common characteristic among people who have achieved a significant measure of financial freedom. These individuals and institutions view *giving* as a privilege and not as an obligation or responsibility.

Thinking back to the best and greatest book ever written about wealth management, consider this compelling quote:

"'Test me in this,' says the Lord God Almighty, 'and see if I will not throw open the floodgates of heaven and pour out so much blessing that you will not have room enough for it.'"

(Malachi 3:10)

Throughout this entire great book, we are discouraged from ever testing God. This passage is an exception. That test referred to tithing—the opportunity, discipline and practice of setting money aside every week to support ministries, churches, charities and causes that are near and dear to us.

For you, it might be signing up for a contribution to the United Way, or tithing (giving a regular portion of your income) to your church. It might be supporting a worthy cause like Wounded Warrior or hundreds of others. One key characteristic I find is that those who achieve significant financial independence also tend to be people with very generous hearts.

And what about those who develop great wealth but don't give generously? Well, the sad truth is that these people are sometimes the poorest of all. Though they may possess great financial wealth, they lack "True Wealth," those many, many things that money cannot buy. But those that give, and give generously, always seem to have a wealth beyond measure.

Financial Redemption

I was sitting in the intersection with my two sons, Isaiah and Daniel, in the backseat behind me. It was an uncomfortable stop at the intersection, because just off to my left there was a homeless man standing with a sign. You can probably relate to why that can be uncomfortable, because just like many people, I often have these internal conversations about why this person is out here. If they can stand with a sign, can they work?—all of those kinds of thoughts.

But what overrode that conversation that day was the voice of Isaiah from the back seat when he asked, "Daddy, what's that man doing?"

I said, "Well, buddy, he has a sign out that says he needs food and money."

Isaiah looked in the backseat where I keep bottles of water and energy bars, because sometimes with my schedule, I miss a meal. He said, "Well, you have food and water. Daddy, why don't we give it to him?"

I had another quick conversation in my head, and the voice I heard said, "Let him give his gift." I pulled up a little bit; I rolled down Isaiah's window, and Isaiah reached out with a bottle of water and an energy bar to this homeless man, and I saw an image that I will never forget. This man, who had a face worn by experiences in life that I will probably never be able to relate to, looked in the car, and as he graciously received those gifts from my son, he smiled and said, "God bless you, little man."

I'll never forget that and neither will my boys.

A couple of weeks later, I was at home preparing for a business trip, and a box showed up in the mail—I don't even remember what was in it. Isaiah later saw the empty box and asked, "Daddy, can I have the box?"

"Sure," I said. He came back to me in about twenty minutes with the box, and it was all sealed up. On the outside, in a bold marker, was written, "To a homeless man."

"Daddy, when you go out for business, I want you to give this to the homeless man," Isaiah said.

"Well, buddy, I don't know that he'll be there at that same intersection." I started thinking of all the complicating factors, and I was not really understanding the scope of what had just happened.

Another thought occurred to me, and I said, "Buddy, may I ask what's in the box?" I thought, "Before I give a box to a homeless person, it might be a good idea to know what is in it."

Isaiah looked up at me with his bright eyes, and politely said, "No, thanks." He did not want me to know what was in the box. Now, I was hoping it wasn't cash or credit cards or something that he sees us use to buy food to eat, but I made him a promise.

So on that business trip, I was at the same intersection where we had seen the homeless person weeks before. There was no homeless person and no sign. I drove around looking for a homeless person to give a box to, but I couldn't find a homeless person. Then, I walked around downtown with the box—which I had no idea what its contents were—trying to give it to someone I could not seem to find.

I finally found a gentleman sitting on the concrete, and I said, "This is a gift from my son and from the God who inspired him."

The previous week in church, our pastor had talked about the fact that sometimes it's better to give than receive. That day, my son illustrated something we refer to as financial redemption. Financial redemption is when the heart of good stewardship is the fruit of good stewardship.

> *We can make life decisions—financial decisions that reflect our deepest core values—rather than sometimes having to compromise on the decisions that we make because we've not been good stewards. Through the heart of my son and a homeless man that he'll probably never meet again, I learned about the idea of financial redemption in a way that I might never imagined.*

The Complete Picture

As you consider these Seven Circles and One Heart to Financial Freedom, it is important that you recognize the interplay between them. Investments cannot survive without savings. Savings often cannot carry us through great financial troubles without the added time and reassurance that comes with insurance. And the heart of it all is critical if we are to have True Wealth, but none of it is possible if we don't first develop the habit of putting money away before we spend.

CHAPTER SEVEN

The Secret Ingredient of Every Successful Investment Strategy

The "secret ingredient of every successful investment strategy" is the discipline and behavior of the investor.

The Holy Grail of investing. Throughout the ages, people have invested great amounts of time and vast amounts of money and attention to finding the one investment strategy that works best. Turn on your radio and you will hear advertisements offering "free" audios that introduce the next breakthrough in investing success. Open your newspaper and you are likely to find ads that appeal to our insatiable desire to "beat the market." Seminars are conducted in hotels to "prove" some new-fangled system works by illustrating a set of circumstances where it performed flawlessly.

And as you might expect, each of these systems comes with an offer: for a modest monthly fee, a significant lump sum tuition or a combination of both, they will give you the keys to the investing kingdom. Some of these systems include a stunningly beautiful dashboard with red arrows or green lights that will provide clairvoyant indications of when to buy or sell, at just the right time. Many of these systems will appeal to your emotions, which can be used to motivate you to sign up for the program.

Have you ever heard any of these?

- Tired of getting taken advantage of by Wall Street?
- Why is everyone making money on your portfolio but you?
- Your financial advisor won't want you to have this information!

Perhaps some of the following quotes from the brightest minds to ever grace the world of investing will provide some much needed perspective here.

"The right time to invest is when you have the money."
-Shelby Cullom Davis

"Diversification is an established tenet of conservative investment."
-Benjamin Graham

"If you are not willing to own a stock for 10 years, do not even think about owning it for 10 minutes."
-Warren Buffet

"Nobody can predict interest rates, the future of the economy or the stock market. Dismiss all such forecasts and concentrate on what is actually happening with the companies in which you've invested. Far more money has been lost by investors preparing for corrections or trying to anticipate corrections than has been lost in the corrections themselves."
-Peter Lynch

Armed with the wisdom of the statements above, let's dig more deeply into several investing strategies and their secret ingredients.

Individual Security Selection

If you choose to construct a portfolio comprised of individual stocks, bonds, etc., there are several critical components you must consider:

- Stocks should be selected for their long-term potential (unless one is engaged in short-term trading, an entirely different and speculative exercise).

- Set for yourself a pre-determined "sell" price. Adhering to your sell discipline to minimize losses is an important commitment to long-term capital preservation.

- Set a pre-determined growth target. If the stock reaches the target, consider selling a portion of your holding to lock in the gains you have achieved.

- The success of one stock should never tempt you to compromise on the importance of having stocks diversified in other areas of the economy.

Active Investment Management

This is also known as Tactical or Strategic Asset management, Market Timing, Technical Analysis or Trend Following.

In this approach, one adheres to certain market indicators to determine when conditions are ripe to buy or sell a security. Contrary to much of the criticism this discipline receives, it does not so much seek to predict the future of the market as it does to respond more quickly to changing conditions in the economy or market. This discipline attempts to employ the phrase "The trend is your friend." Markets or economic conditions that are trending up typically lead to signals to invest. Declining movements will generally engage a sell discipline with the objective of limiting losses and not holding an investment all the way through a potentially devastating decline.

Passive Investment Management or "Buy and Hold"

For decades this has been the predominant approach within the wealth management industry. The underlying belief was that one cannot "time the markets" and shouldn't even attempt to do so. The foundations of this approach involve designing a diversified portfolio with the intent on holding it for the long term (minimum of 5-10 years or until a change in life circumstances calls for a change in approach.) Avoid the temptation to sell when the portfolio cycles through a downturn, or to throw more money at it ("chase returns") when the market is moving upward.

The following illustration is designed to give a visual demonstration of how the previous two strategies might be utilized. Please note that it is for illustrative purposes only and not meant to predict any results that could be obtained with either system

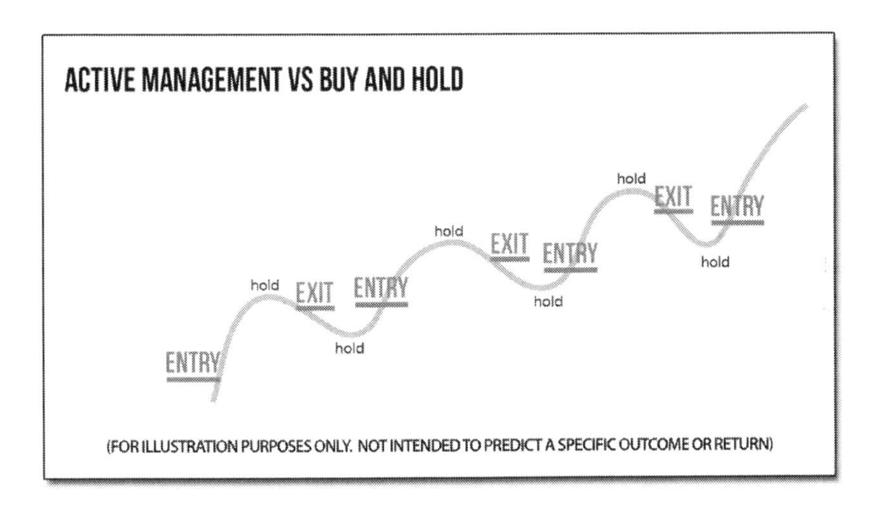

Which approach to investment management is right for you? **The one you stick with!**

When I refer to the "secret ingredient" of every successful strategy, that ingredient is the discipline of, and commitment by, the investor. If you employ the discipline of individual security selection but are tempted out of solid diversification or the rules on buying and selling, you may be headed for emotional peaks and valleys (which lead to more valleys than peaks on your investment statement). If you are going to use the Active Management/Trend Following strategy, but fail to follow the trend signals upon which to buy or sell securities, your failure can lead to the very type of crash that the strategy was designed to avoid. If you choose Buy and Hold but then allow emotion to scare you into selling investments at the wrong time, or greed triggers the temptation to buy at a peak, the "buy and hold" approach will fail to meet its objective of insulating the strategy from emotional peaks and valleys.

The American Funds Group, a highly respected mutual fund organization, recently published a resource entitled, "Principles for Investment Success." While the entire report is available on my website (MyWayofWealth.com), a few key statistics are worthy for this discussion. One statistic is from the annual DALBAR Study, which seeks to compare the investment returns actually earned by investors with the returns actually generated by the invest-ments. We know from historical studies that investors tend to throw money at funds after periods of superior performance and withdraw money from funds after periods of under-performance. For purposes of this chapter, allow me to call this the "performance gap" between what investors earn and what investments earn.

"Over the 20-year period ending December 31, 2011, the average annual return of the Standard & Poor's 500 was 7.8%. During that same 20-year period, the average investor earned 3.5% average annual return."

Why such a disparity? While some may argue that the expenses of funds or advisors may contribute to the performance gap, I would suggest that a significant contributing factor is *the behavior of the investor.* The same American Funds study illustrates that most people tend to invest when markets are at or near a high, and then liquidate when at or near a low. We have taken the investment wisdom of the ages, "buy low and sell high" and turned it instead to "buy high, and sell low."

The "secret ingredient of every successful investment strategy" is the discipline and behavior of the investor. Consider these principles when designing and monitoring your investment strategy. They come from the first and greatest book on finance I have ever read...

"The heart is deceitful above all things and beyond cure. Who can understand it?"

—Jeremiah 17:9

"Cast your bread upon the waters, for after many days you will find it again. Give portions to seven, yes to eight, for you do not know what disaster may come upon the land."

—Ecclesiastes 11:1-2

"Go to the ant you sluggard, consider its ways and be wise. It has no commander, no overseer or ruler, yet it stores its provisions in summer and gathers its food at harvest."

—Proverbs 6: 6-8

CHAPTER EIGHT

The Theory of Decreasing Responsibility

Be careful about the assumptions you make; you may be in for a rude awakening when theory clashes with reality.

There is a myth that many have been led to believe:

Over time...our financial responsibilities decrease.

It goes something like this:

- Our incomes gradually and steadily increase throughout our careers.
- We gradually pay down our mortgages.
- We save for our children's education.

- Our retirement plans systematically earn "market average" (whatever that is) returns.

- Our liabilities decrease, our assets increase, and our net worth grows.

Unfortunately, *reality* tends to clash with the *theory* of decreasing responsibility.

First, though incomes have historically increased as people have advanced in their careers, this is not necessarily the case for everyone or for now. Over the last several years, many people have been forced to accept pay cuts instead of pay increases as they have advanced in their careers. Rather than be "downsized," many people in the workforce have accepted a decrease in benefits, less than full-time employment, etc.

Second, most people just aren't paying down their mortgages these days. In fact, rather than take on one home and one mortgage, many have been lured by low interest rates into second mortgages, many more than once.

Do you have a higher balance on your mortgage than you thought you would at this stage in life? You are not alone. Perhaps you chose to have a spouse stay at home for a season while the children were young. And maybe then you encountered the challenges of re-entering the work force in a fragile economy with high unemployment and even higher "under-employment." For many, the gradual pay down of a single mortgage is just not a reality.

Have you made some financial compromises for your family's quality of life? You may have chosen to send your children to private schools. This investment in their education (which I am not criticizing) strains the budget during the years when we would normally be saving for college.

And what about your college savings funds? Are they where you thought they would be? (I am going to be kind and not even go into the issue of student loans, which now represent a greater liability than all of our country's credit card debt). Have you been able to save for your children's college at all? The rising cost of college (the tuition rate increases an average of 8% per year[24]) combined with the greater financial pressures we are now encountering have become a "one-two punch" on our ability to save for college. Many families are just struggling to pay their current bills, let alone do any significant saving for college.

Now, what about the value of your retirement accounts and your ability to earn "market average returns?" Let's go back in time ten years and pretend I asked you how much money you would have in your retirement savings by now. How have you done? You see, many people have been promised their investments would grow at a "market average return." The problem is that averages are not necessarily stable. While an advisor might calculate a certain projected return over a decade or two, the reality is that such projections are "for illustration purposes only." And the "market

---

24. FinAid, "The Smart Student Guide to Financial Aid: Tuition Inflation." Accessed July 30, 2013. http://www.finaid.org/savings/tuition-inflation.phtml.

average returns" can change dramatically, as we have seen in the last decade.

Finally, there is yet one other factor attacking our ability to increase our wealth and decrease our responsibility: decreasing inheritance. Many of us have encountered the situation (and many more will) where a potential inheritance has been consumed by our parents' medical and long-term care expenses. This is compounded by our parents' inability to earn any reasonable yields on fixed income investments combined with stock market challenges. What in decades past might have become a sizable inheritance has instead been lost to medical bills and poor returns.

Can you see where the *theory* and *reality* diverge into two vastly different situations?

In fact, the increasing gap between reality and theory was one of the driving reasons for the creation of "MyWayofWealth.com" and "Stewardship Central." My decades of experience in counseling individuals regarding their stewardship revealed a few, somewhat predictable, patterns. Many people rarely take a look at their comprehensive financial picture. Some people ignore addressing their finances in an effort to minimize or avoid the stress that might come with a reality check. The truth is, however, that this avoidance behavior actually increases these people's financial stress level.

In part, the financial industry shares some responsibility here. The complexity of over disclosure, confusing language and difficult-to-read financial statements all contribute to the pattern of individuals choosing not to actively engage with their financial picture. Ironically, this may be one area of life where ignoring it really will "make it go away" (your money that is).

Yet, clearly, we are called to be actively involved in the monitoring and management of our financial condition. In fact, the principle has been known for more than two thousand years:

"Be sure to know the condition of your flocks,
give careful attention to your herds."

Proverbs 27:23

"Now it is required that those who have been given
a trust must prove faithful."

1 Corinthians 4:2.

Stewardship Central is a powerful tool designed to make it dramatically easier to fulfill this important responsibility. This technology enables an individual to see his or her entire financial world in one clear picture. Investment accounts, savings accounts, employer-sponsored retirement plans, mortgage information, credit card balances and even frequent flier miles can all sync into one secure and encrypted web site. It is like having your own financial home page. And unlike many of the "free" services that are available on the internet, this site does not take advertising from any company, nor does it share your information with any outside or third party vendors for endless solicitation of products and services. If you find my approach to engage with you about the world of stewardship to be helpful, my full website focuses on financial education, keeping these ideas fresh and relevant to the changes going on in the world around us. In addition, we maintain model portfolios for your reference as you make your own investment decisions. Visit our website for additional information: www.mywayofwealth.com.

The diligent monitoring and managing of your financial resources can help you to avoid the trap of "the theory of decreasing responsibility." In the context of this illustration, I will point out one of my few areas of significant departure from the excellent work of Dave Ramsey. Ramsey wrote the bestseller, *The Total Money Makeover* and designed "Financial Peace University," both of which have impacted numerous families in their quest for good stewardship. However, most people do not know that he is not a licensed financial advisor or planner and has no experience as a practicing financial professional. Given this, people need to recognize that some of his assumptions can lead a plan astray. Here are two of the assumptions that Ramsey has espoused:

- A person should only buy 20-year, level, term life insurance
- Growth-oriented mutual funds can be assumed to deliver a 12% average annual return over time

Let's explore an example of a 40-year-old man who is going to save 10% of his income over a 20-year period. Dave Ramsey's assumptions (which promote the myth of decreasing responsibility) are that by the time the 20 years are over, this individual should largely be debt free (including the mortgage) and have a sizeable enough nest egg so he can "self-insure" and will no longer need life insurance. Let's illustrate:

Let us assume our investor is going to invest $4,000 per year and expects to get Dave's assumed rate of return of 12%. At the end of 20 years, he can expect to accumulate $333,029, IF and only if, he gets an average of $12 return.

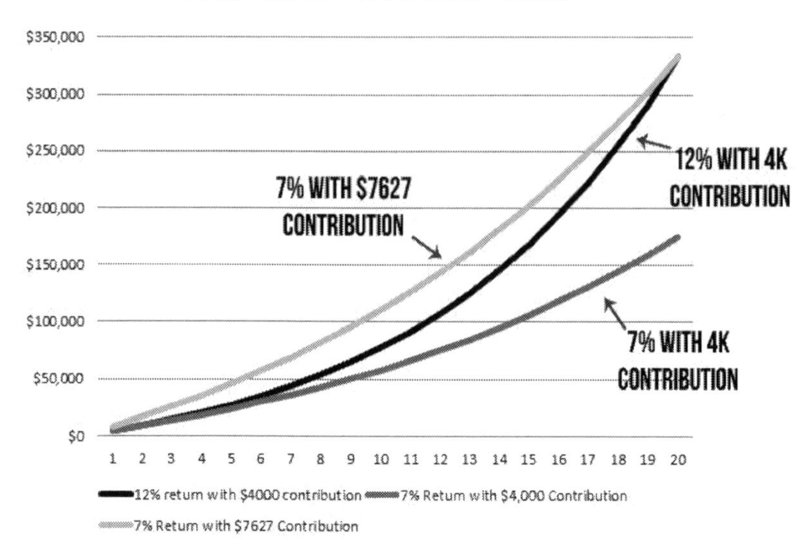

Now, let's see what happens when we change the assumed rate of return to 7%.[25] (as of March 2013, the 20 year average return of the Standard & Poor's 500 was 8.21%). I'm going to use 7% to illustrate the point.

We find that someone investing $4,000 per year with an assumed rate of return of 7% will amass only $174,655. That is a shortfall of $158,394. In order to make up for the shortfall, our individual

25. According to the nineteenth annual edition of the DELBAR Quantitative Analysis of Investor Behavior (QAIB) report released in March, 2013, the average return rate of the S&P 500 from 1992 to 2012 was 8.21%. The QAIB report can be accessed at: http://www.dalbar.com/ProductsServices/AdvisorSolutions/QAIB/tabid/214/Default.aspx.

would actually have to invest $7627 each and every month. This is a substantial difference.

As the above comparison illustrates, the difference between Ramsey's optimistic assumption and an average closer to the most recent 20-year performance of the S&P 500 shows the danger of incorrect assumptions and one of many flaws in the "theory of decreasing responsibility." Investment performance often changes, and people tend to move up in home size and mortgage, not down. The potential inheritance has clashed with the reality of increasing health care costs in retirement and a decade of below-normal averages on fixed income and stock market investments. Those graduating from college with astounding amounts of debt are unable to find jobs and often move back home, increasing the financial burden on their parents. The fragile economy has interrupted many careers and assumptions about earnings. Be careful about the assumptions you make; you may be in for a rude awakening when theory clashes with reality.

Perhaps a final analogy may help drive this point home. When we travel by car, we make assumptions with regard to our fuel economy and the distance a tank of gas will carry us. Incorrectly judging the mileage we will get can leave us stranded. Making incorrect assumptions about how far our financial engine can travel can also leave us stranded. Unfortunately, both situations leave us dependent on others. This is not The Way of Wealth.

CHAPTER NINE

The Only 2 Questions You Need to Answer about Life Insurance

No one likes to buy life insurance.

And no one likes to pay life insurance premiums either, but most of us need what life insurance does for us. Failure to include this in your "Way of Wealth" process can be fatal to your financial plans (pun intended). If you are among the many who don't like to pay for insurance, I have a question for you: "Do you value the security life insurance provides more than you dislike paying the premiums?"

Life insurance is like an investment in a time machine. In the event that time does not allow for the fruition of your wealth management strategies, life insurance is designed to provide for your beneficiaries. Unfortunately, designing the right life insurance solution can prove to be arduous and uncomfortable. This is why I've simplified the process down to two simple questions.

This chapter will help you focus on those two questions and to design the framework of your insurance plan. So here they are:

- **How much life insurance do I need?**
- **What kind of life insurance do I need?**

If you can answer these, you will be equipped to tackle almost any issue that arises in searching for a life insurance solution. Before we dive into finding your solution, however, there are some principles about life insurance you should consider.

Although life insurance tends to be a rather personal matter, it has more than just personal applications. There are many uses and strategies for life insurance which can help us plan our estates and grow our businesses, in addition to meeting our personal needs. I will touch on each of these topics, but exploring them in depth is beyond the scope of this book. Therefore, I encourage you to visit MyWayofWealth.com for a more detailed explanation.

Estate Planning:

Life insurance remains the only vehicle designed to be at its highest value at the very time it is needed most. If your investments are down in value at the time of death and funds are needed, life insurance "buys the time" for them to recover. Access to the tax-free death benefits of a life insurance policy can allow time for investments to go through their ideal life cycle without forced liquidation at a time of desperate need. For any estate settlement costs, from simple funeral expenses to more complex estate-settlement taxes, the leverage offered by life insurance remains incredibly powerful. However, with life spans increasing and the potential for estate settlement expenses to be incurred at an old age, term insurance is generally not a wise solution for the eventual estate planning and final expense costs. Most studies show that people discontinue their term insurance when the premiums escalate as they age. Therefore, the benefits of term insurance are not available for assist with estate planning needs.

Business Related Needs:

The greatest asset any business has is its human capital. If you are a business owner, my guess is that you've insured your equipment, property, vehicles, liabilities, inventory, etc... but the resource often ignored is the people that make a business successful. Consider how the business might react to the loss of a key sales or management executive. Would the business continue to thrive after the loss of an owner? Remember, a written agreement spelling out the details and options for the perpetuation of a business is not worth much if there is no funding in place to fulfill the terms of that agreement. Be careful about assuming that a bank will be willing to lend money to the next generation of business owners after the death of an owner. The ability to secure credit for a business is often a function of the credit worthiness of the owner(s). Life insurance can play a key role in securing and maintaining credit for a business. The likelihood of a business succeeding in the transfer to new owners can be significantly enhanced if life insurance proceeds provide for the elimination of any business-related debt.

A life insurance solution may be as simple as term insurance equal to several years' worth of salary for a key individual. It can also be calculated based on the formula used to value the business in the event of a death of an owner. However, the solution may be more complex. It is possible to acquire insurance that generates cash values that can be accumulated as an asset of the corporation. Insurance can provide supplemental income for an owner or key person (Deferred Compensation or Executive Bonus Plans for example). In some cases, these accumulated cash values can also be used to fund future premium payments, although this strategy does need to be monitored and updated every few years to confirm sustainability. For example, if one assumes that the cash value of a policy is large enough to cover future premium payments when the cash value is earning a 7% return, we may be in for a rude awakening if yields drop to 3% for an extended period of time. If not monitored on a regular basis, you may receive a letter from the insurance company notifying you that either:

a) Your policy is about to lapse, or

b) You need to make significant premium contributions to keep the policy in effect

Although such plans need to be monitored periodically, the variety of insurance tools available for business purposes is incredibly valuable and move far beyond simple term insurance.

Personal Needs:

Having delivered life insurance proceeds to beneficiaries, I have seen personal insurance policies come full circle. There is an all too common response when a beneficiary receives a payout from a life insurance policy:

"Is this all there is?"

Most people woefully underestimate how much life insurance they need. I will spare you the 30-page printouts with charts, graphs, devastating scenarios and the occasionally manipulative tactics used by insurance sales people. Here is the simple formula to determine how much you need:

1. Calculate the amount of income you would need to replace in the event of your death. This is your Income Replacement Amount.

Since the typical American is living on virtually all of their income, I urge you to be realistic with this number. While some expenses will reduce because you are no longer living, generally one should assume that 70% - 80% of your income should be replaced. Work with your financial advisor or insurance professional on the various scenarios involved when a surviving spouse may or may not work outside the home. However, I urge you to be cautious and realistic in making these assumptions. One of the lessons from the Great Recession is that changes in the economy and work force can make it very difficult for a former stay-at-home spouse to re-enter the full-time work force and earn what the wage he or she expected.

2. Once you know what the Income Replacement Amount is, divide that by 5%.

This will give you an approximation of the amount of capital it will take to generate that income for an indefinite period of time. Since none of us knows when we are going to die, we should plan for our income to be replaced indefinitely. This is accomplished by designing a plan where the principal from the insurance proceeds generates enough interest to replace income without eroding the principal amount.

Here is an example:

You earn $80,000 per year and determine that your Income Replacement Amount is 80% of that or $64,000 per year.

Divide $64,000 by 5% and you end up with $1,280,000.

I can hear those choking noises coming from you right now, “Are you telling me I need $1,280,000 of life insurance?” My answer to you comes in the form of a few questions:

1. Do you want $64,000 of income replaced?

2. Can you come up with another way to generate the replaced income that is paid for on a discounted basis and is initially free from federal taxes? Under current tax laws, the death benefits from a life insurance policy are income tax free.

3. Are there other sources of funding for your Income Replacement Amount?

If your employer provides $100,000 of life insurance, you may choose to deduct that from your insurance needs. If your retirement plan has $250,000 in it, you may choose to deduct that amount from your calculation as well.

You may also choose to calculate potential Social Security Benefits and reduce your Insurance amount by a portion of the projected Social Security Benefits. I would urge caution, however, when making assumptions about the long-term viability of benefits currently projected under Social Security.

If we think about this logically, even considering alternative options in the equation, the amount of life insurance we need comes into perspective. Using the formula above, we have firmly answered the question, "How much insurance do I need?"

What *Kind* of Insurance Do I Need?

To help you determine the type of insurance you will need, you will first want to equip yourself with some information. Obtain a quote for level, term insurance that will last until the end of your target retirement age, or at least the age when your children will have graduated from college (and hopefully not come back!). Term insurance is pure protection with no savings or cash value associated with it, and it is the least expensive form of insurance. It is least expensive with regard to the initial outlay or premium. It may not actually be the least expensive in the long term if your needs are of a permanent nature and the term insurance is no longer in effect when you die. However, your first priority with insurance should be to obtain the right *amount* of coverage. You may contact your local insurance agent, financial professional, or request a quote on our web site:

www.mywayofwealth.com.

Once you have determined the cost of pure term insurance, consider if the cost of this insurance is something you can afford. Consider also your short-term and long-term investing goals. Are you trying to eliminate debt, save for retirement, accumulate money for college education? With this backdrop, determine if you may also have resources available to go beyond simple term insurance and purchase a measure of a more permanent insurance.

Term vs. Permanent Insurance

For short periods of time, the initial premiums for term life insurance are less expensive. As such, it is easiest to cover the amount of insurance you require with such insurance. However, there are some advantages to permanent life insurance which may make such insurance a valuable part of your overall plan.

Flexibility

Life plans rarely unfold as we envision. As I explained in regards to the "Theory of Decreasing Responsibility," there are always twists and turns in our lives: job layoffs, career changes, relocations, unexpected medical expenses, responsibilities in caring for aging parents, etc. Term insurance may be a practical solution for the initial term of the policy (i.e. 20 Year Level Term). Once that guaranteed period is over, however, premiums skyrocket. Owning some permanent life insurance can give your insurance program an element of diversification and flexibility to adapt to the changing circumstances that life throws your way. For example, we witnessed two bear markets during the decade of the 2000s that have each reduced some investment accounts by 30% - 50%. Since life insurance helps "make up the difference" between what we have and what we need in the event of our death, owning a measure of insurance that is permanent presents important flexibility. Many policies have options that allow access to a portion of the insurance value before death. And while I am not a fan of borrowing from investments intended for death or retirement, such flexibility can make a huge difference when the unexpected occurs.

Cash Values

Permanent insurance policies typically develop a cash value. But the cash value feature of a typical permanent life insurance policy was never designed to be a replacement for mutual funds, ROTH IRA's, 401(k) accounts, college savings plans, etc. If one studies the history of the development of the life insurance industry and its products, we find a few primary reasons for cash values.

By paying higher premiums than you would with term insurance, you establish a reserve within the policy. This reserve is designed to help support a level premium structure. From an actuarial perspective, our risk of death increases each year. A level premium structure has us paying a somewhat higher premium level when we are younger to insulate us from skyrocketing premiums at older ages.

But this also establishes a cash value of the policy that can be utilized as a type of emergency/opportunity fund and can often be borrowed against at favorable terms. My caution here is that even though the terms to borrow your cash values often appear tempting, the funds cannot be two places at once. They cannot be borrowed from the policy while simultaneously funding the long-term health of the life insurance policy. If you borrow, do so sparingly.

Most forms of permanent insurance (excluding those with "variable" returns tied to the stock market) invest cash values conservatively. These cash values can help one's overall financial strategy if they are viewed from the context of the role of a conservative vehicle. One argument I see made commonly against permanent insurance is that you are much better buying cheap, term insurance and then investing the difference. When I see a comparison of projected returns between such a method and instead buying permanent insurance, the comparison usually shows the excess contributions going into growth stocks or mutual funds. This really is a skewed comparison, truly an "apples and oranges" comparison. The primary role of most insurance values is to provide for conservatively invested cash values. As such, the performance of cash values should be compared with a bond or fixed income investment, not the more volatile and risky growth sector.

Although these benefits are attractive, the finances required to purchase permanent insurance could cause one to neglect other financial commitments and goals. If that is the case, term insurance may be the better option. Take note; life insurance should *complement* a financial plan, not *be* the financial plan.

Before making a decision to include a form of permanent insurance in your plan, make sure that you have an aggressive plan in place to eliminate short-term debts like credit cards, car loans, etc. You want to make sure you will be able to make significant forward progress on these debts before you add permanent insurance to the mix.

Participate in an employer-sponsored retirement plan at least to the extent of any possible matching contribution offered by your employer. If you are under the age of 40 and a ROTH IRA is available to you, you should begin utilizing that attractive vehicle as well.

If you have children and have not yet begun aggressively saving for higher education expenses, start as soon as possible (see the advantages of 529 College Savings Plans and Coverdell Education Savings Accounts).

Only after initiating these other aspects of a financial plan should you consider adding any significant outlay toward permanent forms of insurance. I have seen too many situations where an insurance agent shows a 14-page projection which tells the client that life insurance can do it all: fund college, fund retirement, fund emergencies.... If you include this form of insurance, do so after you are certain you have the right amount of insurance, a reasonable start toward funding your other priorities, and at a premium commitment you can easily afford.

Now that you know *how much* and *what kind* of life insurance you need, you are ready to tackle almost any issue that may arise in searching for the perfect policy. Remember, having the right life insurance policy is a crucial step on your "Way of Wealth process," and skipping this step could slay your plans for financial freedom (pun intended, again).

Important Note Regarding Existing Permanent Life Insurance Policies!

Within each cash-value-oriented life insurance policy, there are a set of assumptions. A life insurance policy is like an equation. Premiums are contributed and earn the rate of return generated by the insurance company for its policies. Expenses are deducted from the premiums and cash values for administrative expenses, agent compensation and mortality costs. If one or more of these variables do not maintain their original assumptions, several negative outcomes are possible:

1. You may be required to substantially increase the amount of premium you pay in order to maintain the policy.

2. The policy itself may terminate. If the premiums paid and earnings of the policy don't keep up with the expenses, the policy can lapse. This outcome ends the insurance coverage and can leave you with nothing to show for the premiums contributed through the years.

This outcome is increasingly worrisome because of the extended period of time where interest rates and bond yields have hovered near historic lows. Many "permanent" life insurance policies were initially designed and sold assuming interest rates much higher than today. If you have not requested an update projection on the long-term health of your existing life insurance policy, please do so. Ask the insurance company to run the projection to at least age 85 to see if it is funded properly. You don't want your "permanent" life insurance policy to die before you do!

CHAPTER TEN

The 1% Solution

If you adopt only one specific strategy from this book, it should be the 1% solution. If you apply this concept, any investment mistakes you may make along the "Way of Wealth" will not prove fatal to your long-term success. Implementing this single strategy will help you prepare for any career interruptions, which are becoming increasingly more common in today's world. These interruptions, after all, should be anticipated and planned for, not hidden from and avoided.

The average individual today works for the same employer an average of less than 5 years.[26] Over the past twenty years, one in five employees had tenure of less than one year,[27] and forty-five percent stay four years or less.[28] Aside from job changes, many individuals in today's society will experience a total change in career field. The resulting financial stress from these events can be cumbersome, but consistent application of the 1% solution will help reduce your levels of financial stress and all of the physical side effects.

What is this revolutionary strategy of wealth management that I am claiming has the potential to transform your financial life? It is the habit of increasing the amount you are saving by 1% every year.

I understand this may sound simple, and its simplicity may turn you off to its power. Please be reminded that financial success is more attributable to mindset and habit than to any other single characteristic.

Let's assume you are currently saving 5% of your income. On

---

26. United States Department of Labor, "Bureau of Labor Statistics: Economic News Release." Last modified September 18, 2012. Accessed July 30, 2013. http://www.bls.gov/news.release/tenure.nr0.htm.
27. Jaeger, David A., and Ann Huff Stevens. "Is Job Stability in the US Falling? Reconciling Trends in the Current Population Survey and Panel Study of Income Dynamics." *The National Bureau of Economic Research.* (1998).
28. Neumark, David, Daniel Polsky, and Daniel G. Hansen. "Has Job Stability Declined Yet? New Evidence for the 1990's." *The National Bureau of Economic Research.* (1997).

January 1st, start saving 6% instead, it's that easy. You may direct these savings into your emergency fund, college savings for your children, your retirement account or any other medium to long term vehicle.

I know you may have an excuse for not being able to save an extra 1% each year, so let me help you with a reality check…

If the price of a gallon of gasoline spikes up 50 cents per gallon, what do we do?

We pay it.

When the price of health insurance increases (I said "when," not "if"), what do we do?

We pay it.

When our taxes go up (another "when," not "if"), what do we do?

We pay it.

You see, the average American has an incredibly high discipline level; we are completely disciplined about transferring our wealth to other people, when they impose it on us. Yet, we are poorly disciplined about taking money from our current income and moving it into our future security.

Remember, the key is that you must increase what you are saving and investing by 1% every year, without fail or excuse. Once you make this an automatic part of your wealth building mindset and habits, you'll be grateful for the future freedom you receive. For an additional resource on this process of automatic wealth building, I highly recommend David Bach's work, *The Automatic Millionaire.*

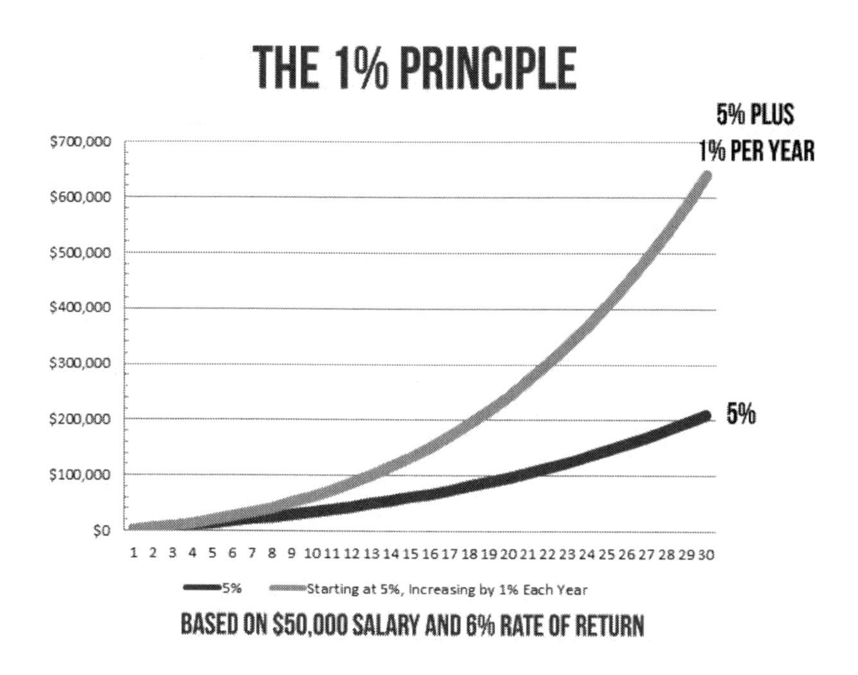

I also applaud efforts by some companies in the retirement plans industry who are now offering a way to automate this process. These firms offer programs in which they will automatically increase the amount employees contribute to their retirement accounts by a stated percentage each year. Of course, this can be changed at the employee's discretion. But here is the key point (reinforced in David Bach's book): absent you "doing" anything, the savings rate automatically increases by the stated percentage on the target date. The key to excellent habits is placing as many things on automatic pilot as possible.

The Caterpillar and the Ant

Never underestimate the power of habits, they often shape our lives in more ways than we realize. To illustrate this, let's talk about bugs…

Caterpillars notably travel in long, undulating lines, one creature behind the other. Jean Hanri Fabre, a French entomologist, once led a group of caterpillars onto the rim of a large flowerpot so that the leader of the procession found himself nose to tail with the last caterpillar in the procession, forming a circle without end or beginning.

Through sheer force of habit and instinct, the ring of caterpillars circled the flowerpot for seven days and seven nights, until they died from exhaustion and starvation. An ample supply of food was close at hand and plainly visible, but it was outside the range of the circle, so the caterpillars continued along the beaten path.

People often behave in a similar way. Habitual patterns and ways of thinking become deeply established. Often, it seems easier and more comfortable to follow habits than to cope with change, even when that change may produce freedom, achievement, and success.

Go to the ant, you sluggard; consider its ways and be wise!

—Proverbs 6:6

The ants that are referred to in Proverbs 6:6 are called Harvester Ants, which live along the Mediterranean coast of Israel. They can be seen working all though the harvest seasons, gathering grain and storing it in their colonies so that they have food to eat in the winter.

I believe a prolonged financial winter is before us. Exploding levels of government spending, uncontrolled use of debt, a lack of sustainability in entitlement programs and many other factors will lead to a lengthy and bitter winter. However, spring will come first to those who have prepared the best, and the 1% solution can be the start of your preparations.

CHAPTER ELEVEN

"Help" or "No Help"? It's Not about the Fee

Wealth management requires a professional's time, energy, research, resources and expertise. You must ask yourself if you have all of those qualifications.

Rick and Sue (names have been changed for confidentiality, but the story is true) had just returned from a meeting with their attorney. The attorney had recommended that they establish a certain type of Trust and make it the beneficiary of all of their accounts, including their retirement accounts.

[DISCLAIMER: I am not an attorney, nor have I ever played one on television. I am not attempting to give legal advice through this true situation. It is designed to illustrate how one aspect of planning where wise counsel is received can be worth years or possibly even decades of fees.]

There are a number of different types of Trusts that can be utilized as management tools for one's estate. In the simplest terms, a Trust is like a box with directions. Assets are placed in the box (either while one is living or upon death). The directions for the box spell out how the individual wishes the proceeds to be managed and distributed in the future. The Trust that was recommended to Rick and Sue would have forced their retirement accounts to be paid out to their children over a 5-year period. I asked Rick and Sue if this was their intention. When they answered, "No" I decided to explain how a concept known as a Stretch IRA works.

A Stretch IRA allows adult children who inherit a retirement account to "stretch" their receipt of those funds over the course of their life expectancy. Given the young age of Rick and Sue's children, this presented a huge advantage. The majority of the funds would remain in the tax sheltered environment. Taxes would only be paid on the yearly withdrawals that are spread out over life expectancy. Had Rick and Sue acted on the advice of their attorney, these withdrawals would have been forced out and taxed over 5 years, rather than the life expectancy of their children (which at the time was over 40 years!) Assuming historically average investment returns, the Stretch IRA Strategy meant over $1 million of additional proceeds would go to Rick and Sue's children. I asked my clients to request that their attorney put the recommendations in writing along with a description of the advantages for executing this strategy. The letter never came.

Asking a professional to put his or her recommendations in writing is a great filter because it places that professional's reputation and reasoning on the line. If you want to know if your financial professional is willing to stand by their recommendations, just ask, "Would you please put that in writing?" The value of my counsel in helping this client avoid a less than productive piece of advice would conceivably save their family more than a decade of professional financial planning or investment management fees.

Now, let's transition to the question of whether you should seek professional advice…

Should you manage your own finances, or seek a professional's help? There are countless articles, books, seminars and expert opinions bent on answering this question. However, having been actively involved in delivering wealth management services to individuals and institutions since 1985, my answer may surprise you…it depends.

The one thing I can tell you is that you should not make this decision based on the fee involved with the services of a professional. The decision to use a financial professional for your wealth management strategy should revolve around how much personal involvement you can handle, not the compensation of the professional. There should be a progression of thought in working through this decision. First, ask yourself these questions:

- Do you have the time, energy and resources to do your own investment research? (No—listening to Dave Ramsey, watching Suzi Orman or being dysfunctionally entertained by Jim Kramer doesn't count as research.)

- Do you have the energy to keep up to date with changes in tax laws, new investment vehicles and planning strategies?

- Can you make sound financial decisions in a non-emotional manner?

Here is the big one…

- What is the value of what you would rather be doing while someone else is managing your money?

There was a brief season when my wife Jen was home schooling our children. I remember one morning when the illustration of this point made such a vivid impression. We had hired someone to help clean our home a few times each month.

As she was cleaning, Jen was in the living room praying with Isaiah and Daniel as they began their home schooling day. I could hire someone and delegate to them the cleaning of our home. But I could not replace the devotion that was being poured into our boys during that season when they were being home schooled.

Let me share another illustration.

Peggy was set to retire after a very successful career. Her husband had already retired a few years earlier, and Peggy wanted me to help her establish a strategy for her long-term income and retirement security needs.

"How much detail would you like regarding the investment strategy we are going to use?" I asked. (Obviously I had the stack of legally required disclosures, prospectuses, etc. that are required to be given to all clients).

She put her arm around her 5-year-old grandson, Josh, and said, "You take care of that (referring to her finances), and I'll take care of this (referring to her grandson)." There has never been a clearer and more compelling illustration of what I refer to as "Focusing on True Wealth."

Although Peggy decided to focus on her grandson and delegated her investment strategy to a financial professional, she did *not* relinquish responsibility. Regardless of who you pay to guide your investment strategy, it is still *your* strategy. Never forsake involvement and control in your financial future. Instead, ask yourself the tough questions and decide how much control is right for you.

If you choose to work with an advisor, there are several guidelines that may serve you well:

1. If your advisor can't explain a strategy in a way that you understand, don't implement it. Even a high level, conceptual

understanding breeds trust. High trust relationships are the ideal for a long term and mutually rewarding outcome.

2. ALWAYS have several ways to validate or confirm the status of your investments. These points of verification may include:

    - Statements from the clearing firm (Pershing, Schwab, Ameritrade, Fidelity, etc.). These statements can be received in physical or electronic format.

    - Telephone access from the firm where the funds are invested

    - Internet access to your account and related activity (the tool we have built into Mywayofwealth.com does this for you…without sharing any of your financial information with outside marketing or financial services firms).

Unfortunately, there has been a common thread in several of the high profile cases where advisors breached the trust given to them by clients. This pattern has existed in cases such as Bernard Madoff and others. At some point they begin manufacturing their own statements for clients. They use their own statements as a substitute for those that should be produced by the third party firm that is actually holding your investments. In Madoff's case, there was an entire section of his office that had restricted access and was used for the production of these fabricated statements. If you ever receive any form of statement or compilation of values from an advisor, always insist on also receiving the source documents. Remember the phrase: "Trust—but VERIFY!"

CHAPTER TWELVE

The Essential Role of FAILURE in Our Economic System

We need to ask ourselves if it is the appropriate role of government to selectively hand out bailouts, stimulus and loans, when "creative destruction" is probably the more suitable answer to failure.

Joseph Schumpeter describes a process that is essential in a capitalistic and free market society. Development and innovation necessarily arise out of the "destruction" of some prior economic order. In other words, "something new and better replaces something older and less efficient." In fact, Schumpeter said that the "process of creative destruction is the essential fact about capitalism."[29] If we think about it, examples are all around us:

29. Joseph A. Schumpeter, *Capitalism, Socialism, and Democracy,* (New York: Harper and Brothers, 1950), 83.

- The first satellite dishes (almost the size of a small room addition) have been "destroyed" (replaced) by dishes that are a fraction of the former size and have better reception.

- Reel to reel tape recorders, VHS recorders, record albums and cassette players have all given way to digital music and video.

- Boom-boxes that could barely be carried on one's shoulder have largely disappeared, being replaced by MP3 players and headphones that fit into your pocket.

- Manufacturing processes have made dramatic increases in efficiency and decreases in size and cost.

With the potential impact of nanotechnology on the horizon, the pace and scope of "creative destruction" may be set to accelerate to levels we have difficulty imagining. So what is the problem? We now live in a dysfunctional mindset where we want the benefits of the free market without the accompanying "creative destruction."

We bail out car manufacturers who are still operating from an economic paradigm where as much as $1,200 - $2,000 of the price of each car goes to unsustainable, union-negotiated salary and benefits. Rather than allowing this model to go through "creative destruction" the government bailed out the car industry and now owns a significant stake, making *General* Motors, *Government* Motors. The systemic challenges remain.

A recent study showed that GM stock would have to triple from its current values for its owners (the U. S taxpayers) to be made whole from the bailout.

We also bail out homeowners who "overbought" by offering them government insured mortgages that avoid the natural consequences of the decision to buy more home than they can afford. Or, the government requires mortgage companies to offer "write downs," effectively forgiving part of the original loans put in place.

We subsidize or otherwise manipulate the student loan debt that is being incurred at a scope greater than we have ever seen. Student loan debt now exceeds total credit card debt in the United States.[30]

Lastly, we selectively use the notion of government stimulus to attempt to artificially manage the creative destruction process. In this way, we throw taxpayer funds at companies that have not yet determined how to create and deliver a product profitably to the consumer (i.e. Solyndra, which we will discuss soon).

Permit me to interject my own definition of a "bailout" for added perspective. A "bailout" is the delay or avoidance of the constructive and necessary lessons and consequences associated with

---

30. de Vise, Daniel. "Student loans surpass auto, credit card debt." *College Inc., Campus life from a business perspective* (blog), March 06, 2012. http://www.washingtonpost.com/blogs/college-inc/post/student-loans-surpass-auto-credit-card-debt/2012/03/06/gIQARFQnuR_blog.html (accessed July 30, 2013).

economic decisions. In bailing-out the automobile manufacturers, we have removed the urgency and incentive for the US automobile industry to adapt to a more streamlined, economic and sustainable cost structure for creating and selling cars. In doing so, we now have a government with a substantial ownership stake in certain companies within the automotive industry. Imagine how this will impact future decision making.

In bailing out homeowners who overbought, we remove the economic consequences that should accompany any financial decision where a person or company (or nation) over extends itself. In addition, this avoids the appropriate return to reasonable lending standards that ultimately serve to protect homeowners from buying homes they simply can't afford under more traditional lending standards.

Historically, any time we make money readily available at little or no cost, the price of underlying products and services increase. This creates a "Bubble Effect" where the prices of underlying products and services increase substantially. Nowhere is this more evident than in higher education, which has been experiencing tuition increases well above the general inflation rate. In some of the recent "Occupy" protests, there are those who believe graduates should not be held accountable for the debts they incurred along the path to obtaining their education. They look to the government to provide a solution (not realizing that the government actually has no money of its own). Again, if we provide any type of forgiveness or lack of accountability for these loans, we may be preventing the creative destruction of the current educational paradigm and the evolution of a more fitting approach to higher education. This could include:

- Greater utilization of community colleges for the first two years of a college education.

- The development of public/private partnerships where large corporations introduce their innovations into our educational system.

- A path through the higher educational system that includes apprenticeships in trades or professions.

- Something other than the current model of a "standard four-year education" that permits students to work their way through college on a "pay as you go basis." (or worse, the "borrow as you can basis")

While the next innovation may be unclear, one thing is certain: our current path of having college students graduate with suffocating levels of debt will severely hinder their financial future and handicap our overall economy for decades.

When the government uses stimulus or bailout money to reward businesses that are not economically viable, we again disrupt the creative destruction process. Inefficient or failing enterprises typically give way to those that are profitable and effective at delivering a product or service to their customers. A recent poster-child for this concept is the failed energy company, Solyndra. Solyndra received $535 million in taxpayer funds as the result of a government (taxpayer) insured loan. Solyndra's problems included questionable political motivations for the loan, as well as pricing assumptions that would have made competition with the Chinese a long shot. Again, we need to ask ourselves if it is the appropriate role of government to selectively hand out bailouts, stimulus and loans. Perhaps a more affordable and less political manner of supporting the development of alternative energy sources would be to offer tax credits to companies and individuals who invest here. In that case, the government would limit itself to creating policy, not picking companies, and the essential role of failure in our economic system would continue. Creative destruction would yield better companies and products.

On a final note, I want to pose a question to "Occupy" protestors:

Would you be willing to give up your smart phone in return for an environment where corporate "greed" would be controlled or eliminated? If one enjoys the benefits of a free market economy (your smart phone), we will always have to clean up the messes created by occasional greed and excess.

Be careful what you ask for. Atlas just might shrug! (If you have not done so, please read *Atlas Shrugged* by Ayn Rand)

CHAPTER THIRTEEN

Inheritance and Legacy—Systematic Contributions Over Time

We must be on guard to ensure that our pursuit of success does not come at the price of significance—a life filled with purpose.

The Bakery

When my family drives past a certain bakery on the east side of Indianapolis, the kids will usually comment about how much they miss going there. It's not because of the baked goods, even though they are very good. It's not because of the location, because it is pretty far out of the way and off the beaten path. It's because when they were young, their "Pop Pop" (their term for their grandfather) would pick them up on Saturdays and take them to the bakery. Their "Pop Pop" has gone home to be with the Lord, but the legacy from the time he invested in his grandchildren is enduring.

In 1982, Tom Peters wrote a highly acclaimed best seller, *In Search of Excellence*. He has since become a widely published and sought after "expert" on the subject of business and personal excellence.

Tom Peters was being interviewed by Steve Farrar, author of the unheralded classic *Point Man*, which encourages and challenges men in their roles as servant leaders of their families. Peters relayed:

"We are frequently asked if it is possible to 'have it all—a full and satisfying personal life and a full and satisfying professional one. Our answer is—NO. The price of excellence is time, energy, attention and focus, at the very time that energy, attention and focus could have gone toward enjoying your daughter's soccer game. Excellence is a high cost item."[31]

That quote sends haunting shivers down my spine. It brings to mind the timeless question, "What does it profit a man [or a woman] to gain the whole world, yet forfeit his soul… (Mark 8:36)" or her health, or relationship with one's children or parents, or time to make a difference in the community?

In Search of Excellence—but at what price? One of the false assumptions that has invaded our notions about handling finances is that it is merely one aspect of life, like an independent spoke on the wheel. I happen to believe a very different philosophy.

---

31. Peters, Thomas J., and Nancy K. Austin. A Passion for Excellence: The Leadership Difference. New York: Warner Books, 1986.

I believe that behind every financial decision is a spiritual core value. Until we make the conscious connection between those two, we are like the dog trying to catch his tail, running around in circles and not knowing why. Think about a great financial goal or conquest you strived for. It might have been a new car or your dream home. Did achieving that goal have a lasting impact on your fundamental happiness? When I ask people this question, the response is predictable. I receive a smile of admission before they confess that it has not made the impact they thought it would.

We continue learning a lesson that was written about several hundred years before the birth of Christ. Listen to the timeless words of Solomon, who had attained great wealth:

"Whoever loves money, never has money enough; whoever loves wealth is never satisfied with his income. This too is meaningless. As goods increase so do those who consume them. And what benefit are they to the owner except to feast his eyes on them."

—Ecclesiastes 5:10.

This passage touches on an economic theory called "propensity to consume." This theory states that the more we make, the more we spend; the more we spend, the more we want to make—and the cycle continues. Solomon's words, written thousands of years before Tom Peter's *In Search of Excellence,* help to illustrate the difference between success and significance. Success can often be easily measured by a balance sheet, financial statement, retirement account, job title, nice car, beautiful home, etc. Significance, while more important, is usually more difficult to measure. Is there peace within the family who lives in that beautiful home? Does the job bring a sense of fulfillment that only comes from using our God-given gifts to make a contribution to others? Is the retirement account simply a means to live a life full of purpose, or is it a dysfunctional substitute for true security?

We must be on guard to ensure that our pursuit of excellence or success does not come at the price of significance. This is a daily challenge in a world where each of us receives thousands of messages each day which promise success if we will just purchase the next magic product or service that promises happiness and fulfillment.

For an extra-credit exercise, make a list of five purchases you have made over your life that did not bring the anticipated sense of fulfillment. If you are like most people, the list could be much, much longer. But look at your short list and think back to what you thought *before* you bought these items. And think about these things now. Are they significant at all?

A popular bumper sticker I've seen reads, "I am spending my children's inheritance." The sad truth is that this is true of our country as a whole. We *are* spending our children's inheritance.

My personal belief is that our children will inherit a very different world than the one we did. Excessive growth of government, woefully underfunded entitlement and benefit programs, skyrocketing debt, an absence of a moral compass and the lack of discernment needed to voluntarily correct course all give me great concern for the world our children will inherit.

"A good man leaves an inheritance for his children's children."

Proverbs 13:33.

For those who have the desire to leave an inheritance for their children (and grandchildren), I would simply suggest you be mindful of the many ways this can be accomplished. The purpose of this book is not to give a lengthy exploration of estate planning strategies. Strategies like "Stretch IRA's" or the use of permanent life insurance to provide an income tax free inheritance are explored more deeply on our web site, MyWayofWealth.com. For the purposes of this chapter, I simply want to bring home a few basics.

First, one of the most effective ways of accumulating wealth is to make systematic (financial) investments over time. Likewise, one of the most effective ways of accumulating *True Wealth,* or creating a legacy, also occurs when we make systematic (time and emotional energy) investments over time. The first investments are financial; the second investments are emotional and spiritual.

Second, be aware of the ways in which some literary works, like the one Tom Peters wrote, influence our thinking. We have become victims of a belief that our financial world and our spiritual world are simply different aspects of the wheel of life. I believe the spiritual component impacts every other area, and the connection between financial and spiritual is pro-found. Understanding this is a key step toward freedom on your *Way of Wealth.*

A PARABLE

Identity Stolen… Character Revealed

Living well within our means: a principle that needs to once again come into our culture:

Gene and Barb (fictitious names) were approaching retirement when they were faced with a family crisis. Their son was going through a very difficult divorce, and their hearts were breaking for their children and grandchildren. Gene and Barb decided to relocate nearly 1,000 miles away, where they could be closer to their children and grandchildren, so they could be more supportive in their lives. Unfortunately, a challenging situation grew decidedly worse.

Gene and Barb discovered that their identity had been stolen and a number of debts incurred. Shockingly, their identity had been stolen by their daughter-in-law! The evidence was clear. There was no doubt about it.

But rather than press charges and seek conviction and repayment, Gene and Barb decided to offer forgiveness. I once asked them what finally led to this difficult decision. They said, "We couldn't put the mother of our grandchildren in jail." They demonstrated how our financial decisions are a reflection of our inner core values. They also reflected what happens when we realize that there are things in life more important than money.

Although Gene and Barb valued other things in life higher than money, they were very responsible with their finances. They had formed the habit of living well within their means decades before this trial ever occurred. Of course, they had no way to anticipate the set of circumstances that would unfold. They were simply being disciplined and obedient to a principle that needs to once again come into our culture: living well within our means.

Gene and Barb's identities may have been stolen, but their character was revealed. The fruit of decades of good stewardship was the freedom to make a financial decision that reflected their deepest values: in this case, mercy and forgiveness over justice. We have no way to know in advance the life circumstances or choices we will face. But this I know—good stewardship presents us with options that procrastination or poor stewardship cannot offer. This is the beginning of freedom and an introduction to a concept known as "financial redemption."

CHAPTER FOURTEEN

The Way of Financial Redemption

Financial redemption is the opposite of economic dependency.

You have heard me use the phrase *financial redemption* at different places this book. To bring home the importance of this concept, allow me to summarize my convictions.

Much of what we know of our world and about money is going to change. The promises that have been made in prior years (retirement plans, union negotiated benefits, entitlement programs, etc.) will face the brutal reality that we do not have the ability to make good on those promises. With the largest generation in history (the Baby Boomers) now cascading into retirement, our ability to pass along this bill to future generations is coming to a demographic end!

Is it fair to those we have made these promises to? Not neces-sarily. Would it be fair to future generations for us to accumulate so much debt in the fulfillment of these promises that their future becomes bankrupt? No.

Certainly, much is going to change in our financial world.

Nonetheless, there is one concept that I would like you to know and practice, no matter what your financial situation is. I am referring to financial redemption.

When something is redeemed, it is restored to its rightful place or value. From a spiritual perspective, I don't believe there is anything we can do on our own, or with our money, to bring about redemption. Redemption, in the spiritual sense, is God's work.

In order to understand my concept of *financial redemption,* perhaps we should contrast it with its polar opposite, bondage or economic dependence. Bondage occurs when we are so far in debt that we become servants to our lender. Similarly, our country loses its ability to lead when we are indebted to other countries around the world. As individuals, our freedoms are limited when we are so far in debt that we suffocate under its weight. A consequence of poor stewardship, this type of dependence forces us to compromise our values. Financial redemption, however, is just the opposite.

The fruit of good stewardship is the freedom to make our financial decisions in a way that reflects our core values. For example, you may choose to leave a high stress job that is causing health or marital problems. Or, you may be able to care for an ailing parent because you've lived within your means for an extended period of time. In a business, *financial redemption* could mean the freedom to turn down any form of government bailout or funding, like Hillsdale College does or Ford Motor Company did during the great automobile bailout. For these institutions, their *financial redemption* was reflected in the fact that their desire for independence was greater than their willingness to accept any form of government bailout or funding.

But financial redemption is not a destination. It is the ongoing fruit of accepting personal responsibility and avoiding economic dependence. It gives us the freedom to make financial decisions that are consistent with our deepest core values, rather than having to make decisions compromised by a pattern of poor financial choices.

My personal *Way of Wealth* was transformed by the experience of holding my first child in my arms. Many of us remember that day our first child was born; the miracle that unfolds before our eyes seems to place all of life in its proper perspective. For my wife Jen and me, that perspective was eternal. When we first held Micah, we knew we would only have him for a short time. Due to some unforeseen complications on the day he was born, his precious little body had suffered greatly and he would be with us for only a few hours.

In that moment, we were reminded that we can see life with the greatest clarity in periods of pure brokenness. There is something in our vision that grows stronger through tears, and our emotions are perhaps more vivid during tragedy as compared with blessing. A broken heart truly is an open heart, and in many ways, our hearts were as broken as was Micah's tender body. No amount of money would've made any difference in a setting like that. The things of this world pale by comparison, while the things of the next world come into full and brilliant view. The grace and mercy of God and the love of family and friends are riches beyond measure.

I have also experienced *financial redemption* in the freedom to walk away from business opportunities or clients that are not the right fit. Family members have taken extended periods of time away from work to care for our aging parents during their last season of life. Even the time devoted to creating *The Way of Wealth* is a freedom that I do not take for granted.

My business has been blessed over nearly three decades to work with, in some cases, three generations within certain families. Our family has grown with three beautiful children; Nora, Isaiah and Daniel. Our home is in the scenic Blue Ridge Mountains of Virginia; we balance time between Virginia and Indiana. We have been blessed beyond any measure.

Please hear the message. Our challenge to take care of our worldly wealth is an important test.

"If you have not been trustworthy in the handling of worldly wealth, who will entrust true riches to you?"

—Luke 16:11

There are true riches that await each and every one of us. They are treasures far beyond any worldly wealth.

CHAPTER FIFTEEN

The Way of Health

"Your first wealth is your health."
—Ralph Waldo Emerson

10,000 every day.

In 2013, 10,000 Baby Boomers turn age 65 every day. This is significant because Fidelity Investments estimates that a retiring 65-year-old couple will need approximately $240,000 to cover medical expenses, according to a 2009 study.[32] The purpose of this chapter is not to debate about a nationalized form of health care as a viable solution. No matter how we choose to structure the delivery of our health care system, the cost eventually works its

32. Fidelity, "Fidelity Estimates Couples Retiring In 2012 Will Need $240,000 To Pay Medical Expenses Throughout Retirement." Last modified May 09, 2012. Accessed July 30, 2013. http://www.fidelity.com/inside-fidelity/individual-investing/retiree-health-care-costs-2012.

way through to us. Rather, this chapter is meant to encourage you to think about your health as a serious aspect in your finances.

After witnessing decades of significant increases in longevity, we may be raising the first generation in history to have a shorter life expectancy than their parents. As sedentary lifestyles weave further into the norms of our society, disease and illness increase as our rate of physical activity decreases. Childhood obesity rates are soaring, diabetes rates are off the charts and cardiovascular disease seems to increase in proportion to the deterioration of the American diet.

Sadly, most of the health problems we face as a nation involve preventable diseases caused by lifestyle choices:

- Approximately one-half of all chronic diseases are linked to preventable problems (smoking, obesity, physical inactivity, etc.) according to Centers for Disease Control.[33]

- Dr. Roger Landry, a medical doctor and president of Masterpiece Living, estimates that the U.S. could save nearly a third of our $2 trillion annual health care budget if we focused on preventative care.[34]

---

33. Centers for Disease Control and Prevention, "Chronic Diseases and Health Promotion." Last modified August 13, 2012. Accessed July 30, 2013. http://www.cdc.gov/chronicdisease/overview/index.htm.
34. PRWeb, "Health Care Costs Can Shrink by One Third if Feds Focus on Preventative Senior Care, Says Aging Expert." Last modified November 23, 2010. Accessed July 30, 2013. http://www.prweb.com/releases/deaconessassociation found/vitalsignsforum/prweb4822414.htm.

- Currently, about 4% of our current health care expenditures are invested in prevention programs.[35]

The truth is that our personal health directly affects our financial circumstances. Therefore, one of the most significant factors along your *Way of Wealth* is the accumulation of health, wellness and wise nutritional choices.

A 2007 study by Centers for Medicare & Medicaid Services revealed that 75% of our health care spending goes to treatment of chronic diseases.[36] When we give ourselves permission to live an unhealthy lifestyle, it bankrupts our health care system. We cannot continue to make whatever lifestyle and health related choices we wish and assume someone else will pay for it. This notion is simply and utterly unsustainable.

The health, wellness and lifestyle choices you make today will have a direct and significant influence on your financial security tomorrow. You don't have to wait for health insurance overhaul. Don't blame your employer or health insurance company for not reimbursing you for preventative medicine. Remember the premise we discussed early on in the book: some people make

---

35. The New York Academy of Medicine, "Compendium of Provent Community-Based Prevention Programs." Accessed July 30, 2013. http://www.nyam.org/news/docs/Compendium-of-Proven-Community-Based-Prevention-Programs.pdf.
36. KaiserEDU.org, "U.S. Health Care Costs." Last modified 2012. Accessed July 30, 2013. http://www.kaiseredu.org/issue-modules/us-health-care-costs/background-brief.aspx.

excuses, others make progress. You get to choose. Your health is your responsibility.

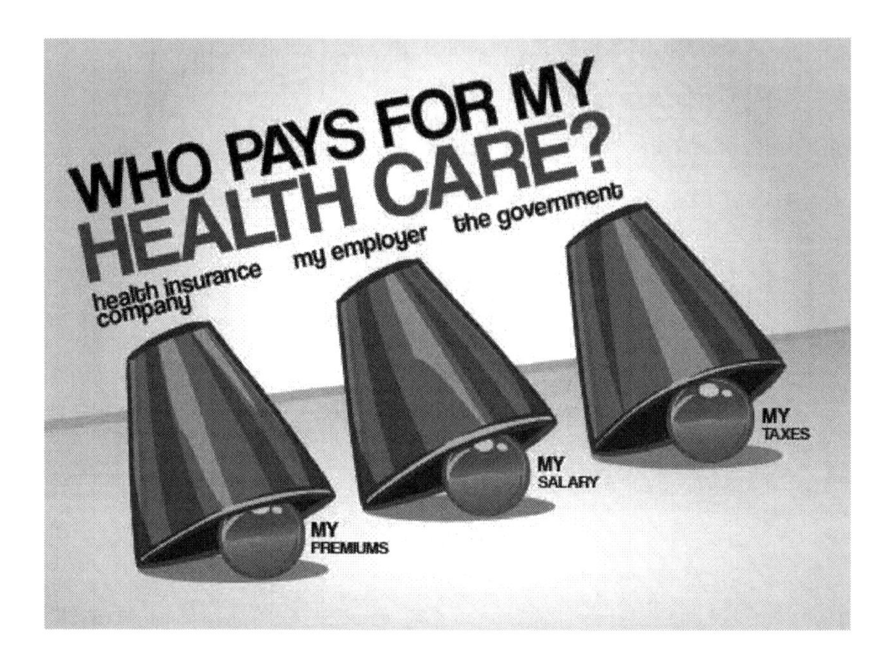

Fortunately, there are many ways for us to manage unhealthy habits. You don't need to hire a personal trainer or pay for an expensive gym membership if you don't want to. Gradual changes to our daily lives can have an enormous impact on our health. Try limiting the television viewing in your home to a pre-determined amount per week. Perhaps you can even discuss as a family how those limited hours will be spent. Turn off or limit video game play and try active games. Virtual play only burns imaginary calories; real play burns real calories. Find time to go for a walk, try out a yoga DVD, or exercise on your treadmill instead of piling dirty laundry on it. Finally, watch the frequency with which you eat out and the choices you make when you do.

The tide may be beginning to turn. Some employers are adopting wellness programs and experiencing great benefits. A 2010 report from the Health Management Research Center at the University of Michigan indicated that for every $1 invested in wellness programs, companies saved $6 in health insurance costs. It may be literally and figuratively true that *"an ounce of prevention is worth a pound of cure" (Benjamin Franklin).*

The cycle of making poor health and nutritional choices, then expecting medicine to fix the problem, must be broken. No health care structure is practical when 10,000 people a day are turning 65 while many Americans are turning their backs on personal responsibility for health and wellness. It is imperative to remember that one of the most essential steps we can take toward our future financial security rests in the health, lifestyle and wellness decisions we make today.

For more on this topic, stay tuned for my sequel, ***The Way of Health.***

Now it is not for me to assume the role of your health care professional—which I am not. However, I have a unique per-spective. I have helped individuals prepare for their future from a financial picture for decades. Sadly, some have avoided taking the steps within their control to strive for good health. Medical expenses in retirement pose a serious threat to all of us. When this is combined with the shifting demographic of people living longer and working later in life, taking good care of ourselves is one of the best "financial" decisions we can make.

A PARABLE

Habitat for ~~Humanity~~…"Divinity"

"This is a true story shared by one of my clients."

He was no stranger to adversity. In the few years I've known CB, he's undergone a total hip replacement and his wife was diagnosed with congestive heart failure and breast cancer. Yet somehow, he lifts my spirits each time I interact with him.

In 2008, he and his wife heard about *Habitat for Humanity* through their local church. At the time, they were renting an apart-ment. They were thrilled to discover that they qualified for a Habitat home. Upon moving in, CB made a discovery that reminded him that, although the home may have been built by human hands, the Architect was Divine.

A group of high school kids were doing some landscaping around the new home when one of them uncovered a key in the ground. Upon cleaning up the key, the following inscription was uncovered: *"God never shuts one door without opening another."*

When they handed the key to CB, it was much more than a coincidence. Sometimes a key unlocks a house, but in this case, the key told the story. This story and others like it are why I see giving as a privilege, not an obligation.

Passive giving (writing a check and sending it to an organization) is great and can change the life of the recipient. Active giving (getting involved with the contribution of your time and talents) can change both the life of the recipient and the heart of the giver.

GIVING TIME VS MONEY

CONCLUSION

Two Futures and the Pine Cone

"Which future will you create?"

I see a future of historic levels of economic dependence. The governments around the world that bet the farm on spending trillions of "stimulus" dollars attempting to jump-start the global economy will find that their bet failed. The only manner in which it succeeded was in laying trillions of dollars of debt upon future generations. From a practical perspective, it will never be repaid. I see workers forced to remain in the work force long past the soon-to-be obsolete notion of "retirement." They have no choice. The entitlement programs that were promised to them were underfunded, poorly managed and raided by governments whose appetites for capital knew no bounds. The generation behind them is not large enough to pick up the burden. Their forced decision to continue working will shrink the job market for college graduates, and the unemployment rate and the "under-employment rate" will surge. Workers who retire with company and union pensions will see them re-negotiated (downward) before their very eyes. Protests will grow ugly—even though a protest has never been known to reverse the laws of economics.

"When your outgo exceeds your income, your upkeep will be your downfall."

Governments living well beyond their means are seeing their lines of credit dry up. The global economy is more volatile than ever. The only commodity in abundance is blame. The greatest scarcity is in accepted responsibility. Perhaps the greatest deficit is not merely in monetary terms—but in hope.

I see another future. This future has unleashed the greatest period of entrepreneurial growth our world has ever seen. Individuals and entrepreneurs have done for the world what no government could ever do. They have reminded each of us that our value is not to be discounted as in some government subsidy that breeds nothing but dependence. Rather, these entrepreneurial forces have unleashed a spirit of creation and contribution that has re-engaged the timeless truth that we are creatures of God with His imagination, creativity and unlimited potential. There is a renewed acceptance that personal responsibility is the only path to freedom. The capacity of the individual to create is far superior to the ability of any government to re-distribute. The combination of a truly global economy and ability to utilize media to connect throughout the planet has revolutionized business and economics. Individuals are free to make choices regarding lifestyle, family, business and contribution because their independence and freedom have been created and nurtured by wise financial decisions in each season of life. The best word to describe this future is "abundance."

Which future will come true? Perhaps a better question to ask is "Which future will you create?" I believe both futures will compete as we come to grips with the responsibilities of economic adulthood. We will not wake up one day and find ourselves in one of these future scenarios. Rather, choice by choice, belief by belief, contribution by contribution, we will create the future of our choosing. Some will, as Henry David Thoreau stated, "Lead lives of quiet desperation."[37] Others will lead lives of bold inspiration. Some will make excuses. Others will make progress. You get to choose.

"Most men lead lives of quiet desperation and go to the grave with the song still in them."

—Henry David Thoreau, Civil Disobedience and Other Essays

---

37. Thoreau, Henry David. *Walden*. 1854.

There are certain types of pine trees that only reproduce as a result of fires. It takes the extremely high temperature of a fire to cause the outer layers of the tree's pine cones to burn off and explode, casting its seeds. The very fire, temperature and pressure that can destroy can also give new life. I believe the season ahead may be like one of those fires. There will be a wave of "Creative Destruction" that will be uncomfortable. Some will fight this process as though their survival depends upon it. All growth happens outside of our comfort zone. Such will be the growth into the future. For entrepreneurs, this will be an opportunity to unleash creativity, contribution and prosperity beyond the current global stagnation. For people of faith, this season will give an opportunity to minister to those who rejected the notion of personal responsibility and remained imprisoned in economic dependence. To whom much is given…much is required. As we take critical steps toward the creation of the future of our design, may we hear the echoes of the voice of encouragement along "The Way…."

and Jesus said, ***"I am the Way..."*** (John 14:6)

"Well done thy good and faithful servant! You have been faithful with a few things; I will put you in charge of many things. Come and share your Master's happiness."

—Matthew 25:23

THE WAY OF WEALTH PLEDGE

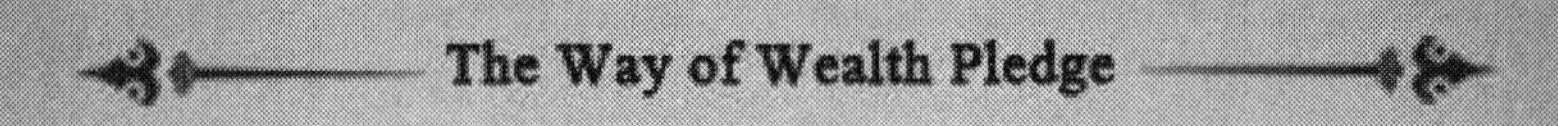

The Way of Wealth Pledge

This is my time. Today is my day.
As all progress begins with the truth, today is the day I stop running from it, or ignoring it...and stand to face it.
With money as with life, I will know the truth, and the truth will set me free.
Today I accept responsibility for my financial situation:
-past / present / future

My present financial situation is not the fault of my parents, my government, my employer, or anyone else. When I blame someone else, I imprison myself. And when I blame myself, I remain in my own prison of guilt. I hereby forgive myself of all former choices and thereby transform any guilt over the past into conviction for my future.

"Each day is a new beginning and a fresh opportunity to be a faithful steward of the many blessings I receive.
Every financial decision,
no matter how small, is a mile marker on my road to freedom.
To reach the destination of freedom, I will travel the road of personal responsibility."

Conditions change, and setbacks arise. Every journey has obstacles and setbacks. They will not derail my path of stewardship. Rather, they will affirm my commitment to it.
Financial freedom is a mindset and daily responsibility.

I cannot control tomorrow. But I choose to influence today and declare that "I am free."

As I pass this test of stewardship through my daily actions, I will keep my eyes open for "true riches:" a moment of laughter, the smile of a child, the faithful love of a true friend, a sunset....

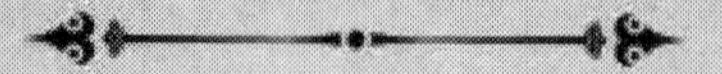

I do not compare my financial situation with that of anyone else. I will not look around in envy but will look up in gratitude. And on occasion, I will permit myself to look back in order to measure my progress. I am so focused on my economy that I refuse to be distracted by what others do with theirs.

I build my wealth gradually, consistently and with risk that is appropriate to me. Knowing that sudden wealth can be more dangerous than poverty, I save and invest with unwavering diligence.

I give a portion of my wealth, not out of responsibility but as a privilege of blessing and sharing. Those who share change the lives not only of the recipient but also of the giver. I purpose to be a life changer. Just as every life matters – so does every dollar.

Money may buy a house, but not a home. It may eliminate my slavery to debt, but does not give my life meaning and purpose. Money may provide an inheritance but not a legacy. Money will be my servant…not my master. Discerning the difference between money and "True Wealth" leads to abundance and freedom.
This discernment will be my greatest resource.

I choose not to dwell on my liabilities but to be grateful for my assets, both financial and eternal. I will live as though the provision for my future depends upon my gratitude for today.

Above all else, I will remember the source of all blessing and provision. He is the giver of all good gifts, including His very own Son.

I am wealthy indeed
I am wealthy indeed
I am wealthy indeed

"Well done thy good and faithful servant. You have been faithful with a few things, I will put you in charge of many things. Come and share your master's happiness!"
(Matthew 25:21)

GET YOUR
WAY OF WEALTH
BONUSES

3 BONUSES!

- Frank's exclusive two-page Financial Roadmap
- "Parables of True Wealth" video series
- Free tele-seminar with Frank!

GET THEM HERE!

Visit www.TheWayOfWealthBook.com/Bonus

About the Author

Frank A. Leyes, ChFC is a speaker, author and financial advisor who splits his time between Indianapolis and the Blue Ridge Mountains of Virginia. A sought after speaker at conferences, workshops, and churches, Frank has developed a gift for reducing complex, sometimes confusing concepts into clear word pictures and parables. Frank believes he has been called to carry his message of financial redemption and responsibility to the world.

As a practicing Chartered Financial Advisor, Frank continues to assist a select group of clients in their personal journey to True Wealth.

Frank lives and writes outside of Roanoke, Virginia with his wife and children, along with their horses, dogs, cats, and more. A deeply spiritual man, Frank is a founding member and deacon of his church.

For speaking engagements, visit http://frankleyes.info

For a wealth management consultation, visit http://frankleyes.com

Made in the USA
San Bernardino, CA
09 March 2020